RAGDOLL REDEEMED:
GROWING UP IN THE SHADOW OF
MARILYN MONROE

Dawn D. Novotny

First published by Dog Ear Publishing
4010 W. 86th Street, Ste H
Indianapolis, IN 46268
www.dogearpublishing.net

ISBN: 978-145750-617-8

This book is printed on acid-free paper.

Printed in the United States of America

Table of Contents

Foreword

IT ALL STARTED when Dawn joined my first online memoir writing class with three other women. In the first phone call, as a way to get started, everyone went around the virtual circle to tell me what they wanted from the class. "I'd like to work on my tenses," Dawn said. "You know, verb tenses."

Here we are, three years later, and what a journey it has been! Dawn has done *so* much more than learn verb tenses. At the beginning of our journey together, she didn't realize what a powerful story she had to tell, which is often the case. In the process of sharing our story, we unzip ourselves and open our hearts to discover who we are, where we have been, and most of all, discover and own the amazing strength and power inside us.

As Dawn wove in the parallels of her story with Marilyn Monroe's, I saw the similarities between their and other women's struggle with abuse and abandonment. Many years before, as part of my studies about abuse, I'd read several books about Marilyn. As I read, it became clear that the losses of her childhood, her confusion about her identity, and her need for love led her toward her life path. In some ways she was born too soon, before the kind of therapy that exists now to help young people who wander lost, abandoned, and in pain. Lost girls often need to find admiration in men's eyes, trying to be "good" so others will approve, confused about their sexuality. They act out in various ways— typical responses to instability and abuse as children. Some can't bear the pain and turn to drugs, and some don't make it, as Marilyn sadly didn't. Though Dawn suffered in similar ways to Marilyn and adopted some of her coping mechanisms, she possessed a unique sense of vision that told her there had to be a better way. "There is more to life than this," she said to herself as she searched for transformation and healing.

Her story shows us all that it's possible to live in the darkness and find the light within. We can follow this light and find our way to ourselves.

Dawn has inspired all of us in the group with her poetic and visceral writing and her tenacity—not only to have lived her story, which is amazing in itself, but to have written her stories over and over again, despite having dyslexia and no background in writing. She not only mastered tenses, she took us deep into the soul of a little girl and young woman who had a unique vision of how life can and should be lived. Her journey goes from a house with no paint to mansions in Hollywood, from being a lost child to finding herself, healing the past, and being able to teach and heal others in her chosen profession.

I am honored to have been with Dawn during her journey, and to have been one of the first readers of her story. At times it was heartbreaking to read her truths, but they were always told with utmost honesty. It was spiritually uplifting to see those brokenhearted pieces and witness the ways her story mirrors a universal struggle: the quest to find a life that goes beyond the sorrow of the past. Her unique story is at the same time like my story and yours—a story of courage. Just as her grandmother repaired the dolls that Dawn rescued from a dumpster, Dawn began her path of self-reclamation. From her story, you will learn how little girls survive abuse and loss, and how a young woman can remake herself into a whole person.

I urge you all to read Dawn's story and learn about her inspiring journey to heal and become whole. Through the story of her life, Dawn offers compassion and forgiveness, and finds her inner compass.

—Linda Joy Myers, Ph.D., author of *The Power of Memoir* and *Don't Call Me Mother*; President, National Association of Memoir Writers

Introduction

*"What I want to tell
is what's on my mind:
'taint Dishes,
'taint Wishes,
its thoughts
flinging by
before I die
and to think
in ink."*

MARILYN MONROE WROTE those lines. No, really: Marilyn did! What *else* would Marilyn have written if she had lived to tell her story, if she had had a chance to do more thinking in ink? What would she have shared if she had reached more often for a pen, and less often for pills, booze, and men? She was ready to talk, to tell us what only Marilyn knew— what it had meant to her to be a mirage that vanished when you got too close to it.

Lots of other people—mostly men—were sure they were what Marilyn wanted. They knew what Marilyn meant to them. She was the leading lady in their wildest fantasy.

I have a feeling that Marilyn and I have a lot in common besides the fact that we shared the same last name—DiMaggio—for a while.

We were both born illegitimately to mothers who didn't want us, and fathers who refused to claim us or our mothers. I'm pretty sure that if we had been born fifty years later, we'd have both been defined as "products of conception." End of story. A pretty short memoir, that.

But we both made it into a childhood in which we were both treated most of the time, and by most of the people in our lives, like troublesome objects instead of treasured human beings.

Before we were ten, we had learned that we possessed something that men wanted enough to become perpetrators to have: our naked bodies. This left Marilyn obsessed with showing off her body to any man who wanted to have a piece of her—even if only in his mind. It affected me in exactly the opposite way: I wouldn't voluntarily give my body away to anyone except the man who I thought would be my one and only husband on what would be my one and only wedding night.

Marilyn and I both learned the hard way that a woman has to define herself by something besides whether a man wants her or not, or by what men want from her. Few men appreciate that kind of self-defining, so a woman has to decide if she's real or just a figment or lust object of a man's imagination.

I think Marilyn was about to decide, but then she died.

I'd like to write a memoir for Marilyn's sake as well as my own. I'd like to write about what it has meant to be spared from death long enough to "put the record straight" for myself. I would like to dedicate this book to Marilyn's memory, and to all of the women who, like myself, are still learning what being a "real woman" means, and to all women who are learning what "real" means to them.

—Dawn Novotny

Don't Cry, My Doll, Don't Cry

Don't cry my doll

Don't cry

I hold you and rock you to sleep

Hush hush

I'm pretending now

I'm not your mother who died.

—Marilyn

I'LL NEVER FORGET the chill of recognition that ran through me when I first read this snippet of Marilyn's effort to express her motherless childhood through poetry. Who can blame her for her confusion? I can't. After all, where else can a child get her first awareness of what life is like except in her mother's womb? And what does a girl-child do if her mother's love doesn't survive the pregnancy, leaving her like a stillborn? I know those may be confusing, convoluted questions, but some girls never know anything but a life with those kinds of questions, and they never find a single answer.

> "Been thinking of my mother a lot lately. I was a mistake. My mother didn't want to have me. I guess she never wanted me. I probably got in her way. I know I must have disgraced her. A divorced woman has enough problems in getting a man, I guess, but one with an illegitimate baby... I wish, I still wish, she had wanted me."
>
> —Marilyn

There is little, if any, shame attached to having a child outside of the sanctity of marriage in twenty-first century America, but in the mid-twentieth century, there was still horrific shame attached to the unwed mother *and* her illegitimate child. The woman was considered loose, a "fallen woman," or "used goods," hardly better than a cheap whore; and the child, whether male or female, was considered a *bastard*.

Marilyn was never able to hide that fact, at least not from herself. Even when she was well along in her career, it cast its shadow over her life.

> "I posed with Alan Ladd for a photo today. He couldn't get over that my mother was a Hollywood film cutter and that my real name was Norma Jeane Mortenson. I never mentioned to him that I was really a bastard child who should have been named Norma Jeane Gifford!"
>
> —Marilyn

Like Marilyn, I knew what it meant to be labeled a bastard; and like her, I also spent the first thirty-five years of my life running from society's definition of our unmarried mothers and unconventional children. The shame of *what* I was seemed as basic as my cell structure, a maternal inheritance.

I guess it isn't really all that great of a surprise that Marilyn and I had such similar childhood stories. Plenty of emotionally unstable, fragile women like our mothers got themselves "in trouble" with men who had no permanent thought of the woman *or* her child. And just like many other fatherless children, Marilyn and I were plagued by uncertainty and lifelong obsession about our biological fathers, even though in both cases they denied paternity until their respective deaths.

Apparently, Marilyn's father abandoned her mother after being told of the pregnancy, just as my father did.

From the day that I finally coerced my grandmother into revealing the truth about my real father, until the day I met him at twenty-nine, I was consumed with thoughts of what he would be like. I was sure he'd want me if he could just see how eager I was to have him in my life. In my imagination, my father held the key to my legitimacy. He was my beginning, the very essence from which I was made. My mother and grandmother had told me many times that I was conceived in love. But I knew if I could just meet him, touch him, and see him with my own eyes, I would somehow become complete.

I also thought that just by meeting my father, I would be set free from the burden—at least in my own heart—of being a bastard. I would be able to laugh in the face of the religious bigotry that declared me forever shut out from God's favor. Thanks to scathing words in the Old Testament, I had spent my life believing that as a bastard I did not deserve to belong anywhere, that I had no legitimate claim on even being a real person. All through my life, I thought, "If only my father could approve of me, I would no longer be an outsider; I would be known and therefore made authentic." From the quotes below, it appears that Marilyn felt similar feelings:

> "Old Charles Stanley would never acknowledge me as his daughter let alone marry my mother!" . . . "All I really wanted from him was to let me call him father.". . . "He didn't want the world to know I was his love child, his mistake." . . . "Oh, how I wished I had a Dad."
>
> —Marilyn

Perhaps this is where Marilyn and I both became convinced that we were not full human beings unless a man's attention made us real. We were daughters of women who were trashed by the men who should have appreciated and honored them as full, equal, and honorable partners. We, too, were cast off as ragdolls, apparently not made of the right stuff anymore than our mothers had been. The legacy of a mother's emotions has a way of imprinting into the very DNA of a child even before birth. It left us indelibly stamped with our mothers' shame.

When you are the child of a mother whose reality is as fragile and easily shattered as were those of our respective mothers, so is your own reality. Thus it was, like many other children with no fathers and minimal mothering, we survived this period, during which numerous adult authority figures entered and exited our lives like so many characters flickering across our life movie screen. And just like the fictional figures in movies, all these people were real only for a brief time before quickly fading out of sight again, always on a stage just beyond reach, devastatingly untouchable. The legacy of untouchable images; images blowing in the wind like characters traversing a stage, people coming and going in all manner of colorful customs, thus binding our self-images to a lifetime of relational uncertainty.

The fragility of our mothers and grandmothers passed a pervasive sense of obligation and bondage from one generation to another at a visceral level, along with many other twisted traditions and confused values we were born into. I didn't understand until I was much older why we felt so obligated to our mothers. There is no greater wound embedded into the core of a child than to be unloved and/or abandoned by their mother. Dr. David Celani, in his book *The Illusion of Love*, cites the work of esteemed psychiatrist W.R.D Fairbairn, who noted "that abused, neglected, and abandoned children were, paradoxically, more attached to their parents than were normal children." There should have been loving eyes reflecting self-worth back to us when we were infants and young children, but instead there were only eyes of emptiness reflecting the tenuousness of mental illness.

I think of how my experiences might have been parallel to those of Marilyn Monroe. How many and which kind of scary eyes did Marilyn have to experience in her beginning and formative years? Certainly she did not have the loving eyes of a father, because hers refused to acknowledge her as his daughter. Nor did she have the loving eyes of her mother or grandmother, for hers were both ravished with mental illnesses, their eyes left with vacancies begotten and compounded by way of institutionalization.

As widely reported, Marilyn's mother, like her mother before her, was unable to maintain employment due to her frequent lapses into mental illness and accompanying "medication." And so it was that, including Marilyn, three generations of women in her family were only able to get through the circumstances of their lives in large part because of the drugs they ingested. The drug prescribed for almost any kind of female nervous disorder in those days, with virtually no thought of its misuse or outright abuse, was Valium. I know, because for part of my childhood, and well into my high school years, my mother lived in a Valium-induced fog that left me emotionally motherless. In both cases—for Marilyn's mother and mine—the use of Valium was probably the only reason that someone didn't die at their hands. My beloved grandmother, herself having been raised in an orphanage, escaped into a continuous haze of Kool cigarettes and her religious obsessions.

Marilyn's mother was taken once again to a psychiatric hospital the day they had to pry a knife from her hands. I was around six or seven the night my mother attacked my stepfather with a butcher knife during a drunken argument. To this day, I can instantly be jerked back to that night by the memory of that helpless reality. I tremble as the remembrance of my mother's insanity threatens to wash over me and leaves me equally unstable. I know by my own experience that a child who is exposed to that degree of uncontrolled adult rage can carry the scars for life and spend years learning how to cope with other people's anger when it becomes even the slightest bit threatening. We naïvely grow up with no sense of internal stability in the face of other people's ire, and become easy hostages to those who would manipulate and even enslave us by our instant fear reaction.

There are many stories of Marilyn having been abused as a child by various people. Marilyn once told her foster mother about a man touching her, only to be disbelieved, and even slapped, for telling such a supposed lie. Marilyn later said that her stuttering began on that day. I do not recall when my stuttering began, but I was quite young.

I know that when a child is molested and has to keep that violation a secret—or worse still, is punished for telling—a powerful rage begins to build inside that child. Some children, even at an early age, can understand when an injustice is perpetrated on them, and they release the rage on themselves with actions like nail biting, or hair pulling, or even wishing to die. Other children act it out externally, by being mean to other children or being disrespectful to parents, teachers, or property. I did several of those things. I bit my nails until they bled, stuttered, prayed to die, and even started a fire. As widely reported, Marilyn struggled with pills, booze, relationships, and whether or not she even wanted to live.

Protracted patterns of erratic responses by caregivers reduce the chances that a child will learn how to regulate their own emotions. Equally devastating to a developing child is the situation of disconnected or disinterested caregivers. It is only through attuned communication that a child learns necessary emotional, mental, and social coherence. It is in the being *seen*, *heard*, and *attuned to* that a child learns how to regulate their own feeling state of emotions. Being seen, mirrored, and met by a loving *other* allows the developing mind to regulate itself.

Remembering how bonded my grandmother and I felt, ensnared as we both were in the tentacles of my mother's sense of entitlement, I often wonder if my eventual marriage at seventeen to Joe DiMaggio's son wasn't a sort of sacrificial offering to my grandmother in exchange for abandoning her. Mind you, this wasn't a conscious thought at the time. I mean, at seventeen I would have done anything to escape my mother's clutches except cause my precious grandmother pain. I was fiercely protective of her. After all, she was the woman who mothered me—who cared whether I lived or died—from the day I was born. I could not fathom facing life without the comfort of her watchful eyes, even if she was without the fortitude or clout to intervene directly in the various abuses other adults—my mother included—heaped on me. I recall years of childhood prayers, begging and bargaining with God to allow her to live until I was old enough to escape. Maybe I really thought that other than introducing my grandmother to Jesus himself, the best thing I could do in exchange for leaving her alone with my mother was to marry Joe DiMaggio's son. After all, for the whole of her life, no one ever loved the Yankees more than my grandmother.

But before that, Hiroshima, Nagasaki, and my childhood had to happen. And I had to grow through a childhood of dumpsters, ragged dolls, and fear.

Bastard Child

"The first pressure of sorrow crushes out from our hearts the best wine; afterwards the constant weight of it brings forth bitterness, the taste and strain from the lees of the vat."

—Henry Wadsworth Longfellow

JULY 3, 1945, curled tightly within the embryonic sac as if I were trying to protect myself even before I was born, my mother's bitterness passed through the placenta to me. Her caustic drip of vengeful thoughts toward the man who knocked her up and then abandoned her for another etched their way into the texture of my being. With an inexplicable knowing, I absorbed the angst she felt around her unwed status. It would be years before I would understand the reason for her uncontrolled, soul-searing sarcasm toward me and my birth. Unfortunately, reasons—even understandable ones—can never erase the scars such hatred leaves. The defacement is indelible; the deformity remains. "Shameful, embarrassing, defective," became the standard by which everyone, myself included, measured me. After all, as the Bible says, "The <u>bastard</u> shall not enter the congregation of the Lord; even to his tenth generation" (Deuteronomy 23:2).

***

Wiping the July sweat from her brow, my mother, Veronica adjusts her burgeoning belly and cries out to her mother, "For God's sake, mother, this child is one month overdue! I can't take this pressure anymore! Go get me what's left of the ice."

Scrambling to calm her agitated daughter, my grandmother, Elizabeth, hurries outside to retrieve the last of the ice from the old ice box on the sagging front porch. She is careful not to step on any of the ancient boards that have nearly rotted through. She smiles at her four-year-old grandson, whose dimples are almost as large as his little round cheeks. "How ya doin', Ronnie?" she croons.

Ronnie glances up, but says nothing in return. Grandmother muses at his overly quiet behavior as he sits on the porch and plays with a collection of broken Popsicle sticks. It troubles her that the child acts so subdued, almost as if he understands the grave predicament facing the family.

Turning her head slightly to catch the hint of a breeze, Elizabeth thinks what a welcome relief it is to be outside, away from the swollen, musty plaster, slopped over broken lath, that makes up the interior walls of the ramshackle old house. Out of sight of her daughter, she touches the rosary beads in her apron pocket for some much-needed strength. The insufferable summer heat relentlessly pulsates on the tin roof, turning the indoors into an oven. What a miracle it would be to get some rain; but there's no sign of any. Elizabeth squints through the heat waves rising from the street into the cloudless sky. It's well past time for the mailman, so there'll be no money either, at least for another day. As she turns and opens the old fashioned icebox, she picks up the ice pick and breaks up the last of the nearly melted block of ice. With the ice gone, there'll be no keeping things cold, but that's okay—there's nothing in the icebox anyway. Elizabeth mentally inventories their entire food supply: two cans of string beans, one can of red beans, half a loaf of bread, and a package of purple drink mix. She hopes tomorrow her widow's pension check will come. It's actually only a fraction of what it costs to survive from month to month, but she's convinced it's how she has supported herself and her two children since her husband died in a construction accident twenty years earlier.

Elizabeth sighs as she thinks of how much she misses the Bronx. Baseball games just don't seem as alive somehow since she began living nearly 3,000 miles from her beloved Yankees. She wonders how long she will have to remain in this unfamiliar place. She willingly made the trip to California to help her daughter in her time of need; still, she feels homesick for the sights and sounds of New York.

Her yearning for New York stops when she remembers the bus trip to Redlands a month ago. Maybe, she muses, she could just put off going home until fall. It won't be so hot then. Besides, going back she won't have to tend Ronnie along the way like she did on the bus coming out from the East. He'll be staying here in California with his mother. Taking care of Ronnie for four months while her daughter settled in California was no problem, of course. Ronnie is almost too perfect, acting mature far beyond his few years. Suddenly she has to chuckle as she thinks of this new baby being so long overdue. For sure, no one is going to rush its coming. "Stubborn little thing," the old woman mutters as she reenters the house.

With the glass of chipped ice delivered to her daughter, Elizabeth crosses the room and turns on the old box radio. Between the hard, discordant sounds of static, she can barely make out the broadcaster's words: "British troops," and something about "DiMaggio." Hunched over the old radio, Elizabeth repeats the news to Veronica: "They're saying that U.S., British, and French troops have moved into Berlin."

Despite the fact that Elizabeth only completed the third grade, her passion for current events has remained a lifelong interest. Veronica, though only able to complete the eighth grade herself, shares her mother's love of world news. An eighth-grade dropout, she still reads Encyclopedia Britannica daily as if every word was a required morsel of food. But today, miserably heavy with child, she doesn't care.

Trying to find something—anything—to break the monotony, Elizabeth tries to make small talk about her favorite Yankee. "I heard that Joe DiMaggio is returning home from the Army. He's sure lookin' skinny, and a heck of a lot older. Darned army life, I guess." Pausing to muse on where to take the gossip next, she continues, "I think he's about thirty or thirty-one now. That pretty blond, Dorothy Arnold, divorced him, you know that? What a shame, having that little boy and all. I wonder if he still has it in him to take us to another World Series?"

Veronica glares at her mother as if to say, "How dare you think about anything but me and my plight." It's obvious—as it always has been and always will be—that my mother expects nothing short of total devotion, attention, and servitude from her mother. And for inexplicable reasons, Elizabeth will comply with her daughter's demands for the remainder of her life—an arrangement that will leave her entirely dependent on her two children for social and financial support. Despite the fantasy that her widow's pension covers their needs, it's actually the other way around: Elizabeth's two children, my Uncle Thomas and Veronica, have taken care of her since their father died, when they were only fourteen and ten years old. No matter how hard Veronica works, Elizabeth still thinks everyone would perish without the godsend of her pension check. Under those circumstances, how could Elizabeth ever leave us? At least, that's one of the reasons she tells herself and all of us over and over for years to come. In the end, Elizabeth will surrender her home in New York, her treasured Catholic church, her friends—even "her" Yankees—and resign herself to living in California.

Eventually, this arrangement will cost Elizabeth her relationship with my Uncle Thomas, who will sever all contact with her to punish her for abandoning him in favor of my mother. If only he could realize how tightly my mother's self-pity can bind those who long to love her and be loved by her, maybe he could understand my grandmother's "choice."

After a few more minutes of trying to hear through the static of the old radio, Elizabeth turns it off. The sullen scowl on Veronica's face shows that her effort at small talk is not appreciated. She goes outside for another breath of air as her next door neighbor, Lucy, delivers some produce.

"Afternoon, Elizabeth," Lucy says, smiling. "Thought you might like these. We've got enough to go around." As she sees the two over-ripe avocados and six figs that Lucy is offering her, tears of gratitude well up in Elizabeth's eyes. She knows she doesn't have to explain or feel embarrassed by her reaction. A lot of people are strapped; WWII drags on. Neighbors share anything they can spare with each other.

After a few minutes of chit-chat and thanks, Elizabeth waves good-bye to Lucy, stands for a moment, and looks out across the neighborhood. Young women left alone by the war occupy almost all the houses. Some wait nervously for their husbands to return, while others—left widowed and alone with young children to raise—try to accept their loved one's death. The prevailing atmosphere of fear and bitterness can be felt everywhere.

Just last week, in their small neighborhood market, Elizabeth noticed two soldiers who had just returned home. They both seemed to look right through her, as if they were staring into a vat of black nothingness. Not able to understand how soldiers who were safe at home could look so lost, she prays for them. She wants to tell them all to trust in God—that He has everything under control. Nobody knows yet that in just barely a month Japan will finally concede defeat after being devastated by the atomic bombs dropped on Hiroshima and Nagasaki.

Back indoors, Elizabeth finds Veronica slumped on the couch. Her torn and soiled muumuu is pulled up around her thighs as she tries to fend off the heat exhaustion that threatens to drive her insane. After all, she's working on being *ten months* pregnant! As another pain pierces through her back, she cries out to her mother, "For the love of God, when will this pregnancy end?"

Returning from putting the produce in the kitchen, Elizabeth holds a cigarette in her left hand and her rosary beads in her right. She might not have been able to tell those two soldiers what she was sure God wanted everyone to hear, but she has a captive audience in her daughter. "Veronica, where is your trust? I mean, look, we're almost out of food and here Lucy brought us some avocados and figs. I tell you, Veronica, God always knows of our needs. Remember where in the Bible Samuel says, "The God of my rock; in him will I trust: he is my shield, and the horn of my salvation, my high tower, and my refuge, my saviour; thou savest me from violence." For Elizabeth, a verse of scripture validates everything.

Flinching as another pain pushes through her now-aching back, Veronica's face drips with misery. "Mother, if you don't stop talking that Bible stuff, I'm tellin' ya, I'm going start screamin'."

As if Veronica hadn't said a thing, Elizabeth plops herself down on the far end of the couch and goes right on: "As for God, his way is perfect; the word of the Lord is tried: he is a buckler to all them that trust in him."

Tightening her fists into balls of rage, Veronica keeps her word and begins to scream. "God damn it, mother, shut up!" Elizabeth's chin quivers as smoke from her cigarette crawls around her sweaty face and fills the air between her and Veronica. She begins coughing violently, and gets up and moves to sit at the old card table that serves as a place to eat and her holy altar. She shakes out the embroidered scarf—a gift from her favorite nun, Sister Veronica—and replaces it beneath the wood crucifix. Next, she snaps on her Lady of Fatima night-light and opens her Bible, a move she hopes will leave her daughter feeling guilty for her sharp tongue and lack of faith.

Despite Veronica's lack of faith—by Elizabeth's standards, at least—less than twenty-four hours later, at the crack of dawn on July 4, she is finally delivered of a 10 pound, 4 ounce baby girl. I'm not sure if she wanted to give me a name to match my size or the length of her pregnancy when she filled out my birth certificate. Nevertheless, she names me Veronica Dawn Nadeau Laskavitch.

Seven days later, weak and anemic, my mother is finally released from the hospital. It was a rough delivery, to say the least, and for the next month she is completely bedridden. While recuperating, Veronica vows she will find a way to remove the bastard stain from this child she has suffered so much for to bring into the world.

Endless tales prevail about what a horrible ordeal the experience was for my mother. The most often-repeated version describes how I was born right in the hospital bed with no doctor in attendance, and how the delivery ripped my mother open, causing her to lose massive amounts of blood. Of course, with my mother unable to care for me, my grandmother would step in to take her place—a situation that never changed for the rest of my life.

The House with No Paint

WHEN I WAS five months old, Mom found a way to move us all from Redlands to San Diego, where she deliberately set out to meet and marry a handsome sailor. Mom was attractive, with her long, chestnut brown hair, sapphire blue eyes, and porcelain skin, and she looked younger than her thirty-two years. In no time, she had done just what she intended, with one small difference—he was an ex-soldier, not a sailor. Howard T. Kelley had striking, blue-black, wavy hair, and eyes so dark you couldn't tell the pupils from the irises. Eyes of coal and choking hands—those would eventually become the most predominant recollections of the only legal father I would know for the first ten years of my life.

An old Army base barrack was converted into an eight-hundred-square-foot home. The house was partitioned into three bedrooms: one for my parents, one for my two brothers, and the third for my grandmother and me. It was so small that when we sat on our twin beds, our knees touched. The Army built the neighborhood barracks so close that everyone could hear their neighbor's conversations, even when they were inside. Most neighbors made their homes pretty with paint, grass, and flowers. Not us! Our house had no paint, no grass, no flowers. Instead, it was littered with broken beer bottles, a big old door lying in the driveway, and dirt. Plain, old, ugly dirt.

As a little girl, I'd daydreamed I lived in the house next door. In size and shape, it was just another little box house, identical in construction to ours, but it was different. The way it showed itself off, the way I imagined it smelled, the way it sounded with happy family sounds, the way it *felt*. The people who lived there planted sweet peas, but could never enjoy them the way I did. When I sat among their flowers, I often imagined that I was at a wonderful party—maybe even a *birthday* party—maybe even *for me*. Sometimes I even ate the flowers. They made me giggle. The flowers felt like a hug in my mouth all the way to my tummy. The blue ones tasted best.

The sweet peas that entwined their arms through the chain link fence that marked the border between plain dirt and manicured lawn next door beckoned to me. Although I was not yet old enough to attend school, I couldn't resist repeating my grandmother's favorite expression for all things really bad or really good when I saw them: "Jesus, Mary, and Joseph." How good those flowers smelled and *tasted*. Their heavenly scent carried me through many a frightening and lonely day as I snuggled in between their leaves and tendrils. I'd often sit there and pretend I was hidden from all the ugliness of my life.

Joining me daily were a handful of tattered dolls found on my scavenging forays behind the local five-and-dime and grocery store. Even though the black Dempster dumpsters sat like towering monsters with their backs against the store walls, I climbed up on old crates or tires and into their cavernous bellies. There, if I was really lucky, I would find discarded candy and other edibles, like stale doughnuts, packages of broken cookies, and overripe fruit. I was content to fill my tummy with any type of food and my arms with soft treasures to hold.

***

My mother—God bless her—couldn't carry through on many things. She couldn't hold her temper, a husband, or a job. Maybe it was failing to marry my real father that made her so determined to never fail again at landing a husband. She made a vow even before I was born, that she would find me a father and make me legitimate. My older half-brother, Ronnie, had been born with a proper heritage: two married parents. Unfortunately, he also never got to know his dad, who died in the war.

My mother was never much of a parent at any stage of my life. But one thing she was able to do without fail was *find* men to marry her. Of course, no one knew what the future would bring when Howard and Veronica married, and I'm sure my mother wasn't thinking that far ahead. All that mattered to her was that Howard was willing to marry her and legally adopt Ronnie and me. In her mind, the inherent evil of her illicit sexual experience with my father would be erased now that she was again married and I had a legal father's name.

They were married when I was ten months old, twenty months after my conception. My birth certificate was to read "Veronica Dawn Nadeau Laskovitch Kelley." In one act, a belated marriage, my mother had, to the world, redeemed herself from whoredom, redeemed my grandmother from having a bastard grandchild, and, of course, redeemed me from being the cursed bastard they all regretted.

I don't think she ever gave a thought to what Howard might be hiding behind his coal-black eyes. No one thought about post-traumatic stress disorder in those days. A man just went to war, waded through his buddies' blood and guts, killed the men who killed his friends, and then, without fanfare, came home and started a family. To the government and society, this was a simple sequence. No one considered the potential ramifications of witnessing the horrors of war. In Howard's case, coming home also involved adopting two other men's fatherless children. At the time, everything seemed just fine—at least, it did to Veronica. Howard not only made her "an honest woman" again, he also never initially appeared to judge her for her "sin." There was even a bonus: he was the best lover she had ever known, a fact she disclosed to me many years later.

Howard was a short man with a board-straight back. But those eyes of his looked right through people, hauntingly, as if there were no soul behind them. He was just twenty-four years old in 1946 when he met and married my mother; he kept his agreement with her, and immediately adopted four-year-old Ronald and ten-month-old me. Two years later, my mother would bear their only child together, Russell.

Howard also inherited my grandmother. Like a barnacle, Elizabeth was permanently attached to her daughter's life, embedded in her very existence. Not long after the marriage, what quiet had existed in the house was gone, and it was a condition that lasted for years. Too little to understand the sheer volume that bellowed from our dingy house, I hung my head in shame when the children playing outside gawked at the noise. The neighbors simply closed their doors or turned their heads from the earsplitting arguing.

Sometimes, when the meanness got too loud, my grandmother squeezed her eyes tighter and tighter and muttered the rosary. Her lips moved as she recited silent words of hope and faith. Her trust never seemed to waver. Rocking back and forth on my bed, staring at the huge wooden Jesus crucifix hanging on the wall, I wondered about Jesus' parents, the Lady of Fatima night-light, and Grandma's prayer book. No matter how tightly she closed her eyes or held her rosary beads to her heart asking Jesus to intercede, her prayers didn't seem to quiet the reverberating sounds.

I often exclaimed, "I hate them. I hate them. I HATE them!" and placed my hands over my ears, trying to prevent the loud, ugly sounds in the next room from ringing through my head and shaking my whole body.

My grandmother shushed me, "Dawnie, Dawnie, they will hear you. You must be very quiet."

Gulping down sobs, I could see the fear in her eyes as she handed me rosary beads from the altar wedged between our twin beds. The rosary beads comforted my grandmother like a pacifier would a small child, while I wanted to smash the beads into a thousand tiny pieces.

When the meanness got really bad and the fighting was louder than usual, and violence seemed surely in the offing, my big brother Ronnie would stuff some bread into my pockets and send me out to the nearbywoods. Once there, I'd climb up into the strong, smooth, round arms of my favorite old eucalyptus tree. Often Ronnie found me there sound asleep, and was puzzled by my ability to balance on my favorite branch. No one could explain why I never fell.

It's true, the sticky trunk sap was partly to blame for my filthy feet, but still I loved to see it clinging between my toes. Strangely, it reminded me of how warm my heartfelt when I saw lipstick on another child's cheek at school. No amount of wishing ever got me any lipstick kisses on my face. That's okay, I thought while sticking my chin out with a bit of smugness. Goodbye kisses made with lipstick weren't any better than goodbye kisses made of sap—they were just higher up on the body.

That eucalyptus was my friend in other ways, too. I could make a blanket from the flat, long pieces of bark, or little playthings that would entertain me for hours. That was something you couldn't do with lipstick kisses left by parents who sent you off to school. I was always careful to only pull off the bark that was hanging loose and about to come off on its own. I didn't want to hurt my tree by pulling off any part that was firmly stuck to its body. I was sure the trees in those woods had feelings, just like mine, and I knew that I wouldn't want someone pulling any skin off of me that wasn't ready to fall off.

This gypsy lifestyle of roaming the woods and the neighborhood was a daily ritual from the time I was barely four years old. From sun-up until well past dark, I was on my own in my wanderings. Sometimes I would seek shelter in the hot afternoons by sneaking into an abandoned barrack. Many had not yet been converted to homes, and it was easy to break into broken doors or holes punched in the walls by vandals. But most of my comfort came from the exhilaration I felt when supported in the loving arms of my trees. No one, except my brother, ever questioned my whereabouts or went looking for me. Usually he didn't come, either, because we both knew the farther I stayed away from the house with no paint, the safer I would be.

Even hunger didn't make me feel like going home. Much safer to check out the latest contents of the dumpsters where foodstuff was abundant. Dumpster "storage" also provided the remains of broken dolls, dolls waiting for some loving hands to rescue them. I'd take them to my grandma. While sitting on her bed beneath the altar where her Jesus, Mary, and Joseph statues stood, she'd clean the dolls, mend them as best she could, and baptize them with a sprinkle of the holy water that the priest brought to bless her with every Friday when he came to the house to give her Holy Communion.

That holy water and those statues, as well as her Bible, gave continual comfort to Grandma, just as the arms of the eucalyptus trees gave continual security to me. To her, they meant God loved her. All things were bearable to my grandmother if she could just see the eyes of Mother Mary—just like I knew that as long as there were soft curls of eucalyptus bark and sweet peas to nestle into, I'd be okay.

This willingness to believe had skipped my mother, though. She could not seem to see past all the things that had infused her life with worry and bitterness. But my grandmother had only one approach to life—to accept God's will in all things, the result of the teaching and influence of Sister Veronica, the head nun at the orphanage where Grandma was raised from age four. I'd someday come to see this quality in her as both her greatest strength and her greatest weakness. But as a child, sharing the same bedroom with her, I found her faithful nightly prayers and scripture reading as comforting as my beloved outdoors.

***

One day while napping I overheard ten-year-old Ronnie speaking in soothing tones to our four-year-old brother Russell. As often happens with the oldest child, Ronnie had become responsible for protecting Russell and me from the screaming matches. The fights between Howard and my mother were escalating in tone and regularity.

I was pretty sure the reason that I was not welcomed into any of the neighbor's homes was because the whole neighborhood could hear the verbal battles in our house. That and the sap on my feet, the lice in my hair, and the dirt from the dumpsters. In spite of any prayers and wishes from Grandmother and me, the hollering became more and more intense.

My mother screamed, "We don't got no food again, Howard! Why the hell don't you apply for that job with more pay?"

"Will you shut up about that goddamn job, Veronica? I like sweeping the floors at the machine shop!" Howard shouted. "Why can't you just leave me alone?"

Mom's voice rose in pitch. "Because we are hungry and I can't pay the bills. Why are you so stubborn and selfish about sweeping stupid floors like some kind of backward idiot? Who the hell likes sweeping floors, anyway?" Then her voice lowered, and dripping with contempt she snapped, "What kind of man are you, anyway?"

The vicious stab found its mark, and Howard roared, "The kind of man that married you, you bitch. Who else would accept a four-year-old boy and bastard baby girl while saving your ass from shame and starvation?"

Not understanding his words, I still cringed under the lash of his bitterness towards Ronnie and me; but he wasn't through yet. He had more to shame my mother with. "Then there's your mother. That god-damn leech never leaves the house and slinks around here like some kind of whipped dog. She's nothing but a freeloader—same as you, Veronica. I'm sick of it all, do you hear me, you stupid, useless woman?"

Forgetting the original spark that started this latest battle, my mother took up the defense of her mother. "Why wouldn't she hide from you, you're nothing but a bully. Last week you beat her up and threw her off of the front porch. The whole neighborhood seen it. I hate your guts and everyone in this house hates your guts. You're a good-for-nothing fool. All you care about is your whiskey. If you ever put your hand on my mother or these kids again, I swear to God, I'll kill you!"

"That bottle is the only thing that I do care about, you crazy bitch. Put down that goddamn knife before I break your arm!"

Terrified, I couldn't sit still any longer. I came out of the bedroom, my knees so wobbly I could hardly walk, just in time to see my mother throw a knife that narrowly missed Howard's head. I peed my pants, which disgusted them both. Howard yelled, "Oh for Christ sakes, what is wrong with this kid?"

Mother screeched at me, "Clean up that mess and get out of my sight, NOW! I don't want to set eyes on you one more time today, do you understand me?" Ashamed, I skulked away.

Howard's face was dark with rage; he retreated to the garage where he kept his liquor stash. Mom withdrew to the dark sanctuary of her bedroom until the next day, or maybe even the next week. I didn't want to see her or know what she was going to do. I avoided going near her, in part because I knew how her eyes would look at me: with an ice-cold stare of hatred that shriveled my insides.

Reverence and Milk Bottles

HOWARD, MY ADOPTIVE father, frequently locked me in my brothers' small bedroom with its colorful floors. One small window became my salvation: I would imagine myself flying out of it to perch upon the fluttering leaves I could see from my assigned square on the floor. It was hard for my four-year-old arms and legs to remain still for so many hours. When he was angry, Howard would frequently grab me by one arm and yank me high up in the air. On one occasion he dislocated my arm from my shoulder before slamming me down on the orange and blue linoleum. For years I had recurring nightmares in which I was frantically running from pieces of orange and blue squares.

Teaching the skills Howard thought I should know began like this: "Now you listen to me, young lady, you are not coming out of this room until you learn to tie those goddamn shoelaces. If I come in here and see that you have moved from that space," (meaning one small portion of the orange and blue squares), "you will be sorry. Do you understand me?"

Sobbing, nodding my head up and down, I tried over and over to master the new task. I so wanted to tie my shoes, but couldn't make the laces stay where I put them. I thought that if I could just be "gooder," then I could make his "mad" go away. Even more than his mad, I wanted to stop his fearsome, coal-black eyes from glaring at me and raising goose bumps on my arms and legs. Pictures of Frosty the Snowman can still make me shudder because his eyes are flat and without pupils, and they give the appearance of death watching through the eyes. That's how I felt; that Howard looked *through* me without looking *at* me. It reminded me of how I felt when looking at the eyes of a dead animal, like death was watching back at me.

After a short time the bedroom door would fly open and Howard would stare at me with that look. Holding my breath, I'd try to become invisible to avoid the piercing fierceness of those eyes. I trembled as he grabbed my neck and picked me up as if I were a toothpick. No words came out of his mouth as he twisted my head one way and my body the other. As suddenly as it started, he dropped me back onto the linoleum and walked out of the room, quietly closing the door behind him. Like an exploding grenade, his act of violence seemed to release the pressure of the anger festering inside of him.

I soon learned that one way to endure his outbursts was to back way up inside of myself as close as I could get to my backbone. If the inside was tucked far away it didn't hurt so much when the outside of me was being twisted around like a broken rag doll. Going limp also made things hurt less. Every time Howard smeared dog poop in my face, I would practice making my insides really small, like a tiny little ball. Eventually, I learned to get small and limp at the same time. I even learned how to breathe without allowing my chest to move. No movement, no sound. Nothing for anyone to notice or hurt—like an animal playing possum.

I suppose poverty was the deciding factor that ultimately forced Mom to choose between sending me to a safe place and getting rid of Howard. She faced what for her must have been a hard choice, since Howard was her income source. She finally sent me eight hundred miles away to San Francisco to live with a childless couple she knew from New York. They had known my biological father, Roland, when he had served in the military. The memory of the day I was sent away has remained extremely vivid. Sometimes the painful feelings return as if it were yesterday.

***

Even my sweet eight-year-old brother couldn't talk me out of the corner where I scrunched up against the wall, hiding, my eyes tightly shut. Holding out his hand to me, Ronnie said, "Come on, Dawnie, these are nice people and they are going to take you for a ride in their big car."

I shook my head from side to side, too scared to talk, and my brother begged me, "Please Dawnie, just come say hi to them. They have a baby doll for you in the car and some candy. I saw it. Everything will be okay. Just come out, pleeeease."

I opened my eyes and saw that my grandmother had one hand over her mouth, as if to prevent fear from tumbling out, while she clutched her rosary beads in the other. It was then that I knew something really bad was happening. Mom's eyes darted around the room like they did just before she started yelling—another bad omen.

From my favorite hiding place beneath the corner table in the living room, I could see this new man standing tall as the sky. He remained silent, nervously twirling his hat in his hand. Suddenly, the beautifully dressed woman was hugging my grandmother like I had watched old friends do in other families.

I could tell that my brother was about to start crying, something he rarely did. I would do anything to keep him from being sad, so I put my hand in his.

As he picked me up, I buried my head into his shoulder, wrapping my legs around his waist and holding onto him with all of my might. He walked out of the front door and stopped beside the big blue car. Someone was trying to pull me loose, but clinging to him, I screamed over and over again, "No, no, no, no, no!" I felt his tears on my face as I was wrenched from his arms. He turned and ran away. I was screaming, "I want Ronnie, I want Ronnie, I want R-o-n-n-i-e!"

***

Except for the empty place in my heart that belonged to my brothers, I thrived in the care of my foster parents. I was never hungry. I loved that everyone smelled so perfumy, like Lux soap. The house had paint and flowers in the yard, no dog poop was put in my face, and they even tied my shoelaces for me.

Every morning, "Mommy" Blanche made me cinnamon toast and a glass of orange juice. Late afternoons, she gently bathed and dressed me in soft little dresses with bows in my hair and black patent leather shoes. I liked to sit near her while she combed her thick salt-and-pepper hair before dabbing lipstick and powder on her pretty face. Then we waited together on the front porch for the man as tall as the sky to walk through the gate. When I would run to him, he would pick me up high over his head, then hug and kiss me, which always made me giggle with delight. Later we would all sit down at a real table and share our dinner, something I had never experienced before. I loved everything about my new home, although I would often think of my big brother and ache for the boy with the dimples who made my heart open wide with smiles.

At my new mom and dad's house, I was not permitted to climb trees, and I had to wear shoes that made my feet feel trapped. But my new parents made me very happy, and I adjusted well.

Later, I was told that they begged my real mom to let me stay with them, but she refused. Without warning or explanation, my mother demanded that I be returned, although nothing had changed at the old house.

One gloomy northern California day, after six heavenly months of peace, my foster parents packed me in their car and headed back to the house with no paint. Nothing my kind new dad or my wonderful new mom said to me could cheer me during the long drive south. Our mutual sadness enveloped the inside of the car like a black fog, becoming denser with each passing mile. Soon no one was even attempting to speak cheery, meaningless words of comfort.

As I got out of the car, I plastered my body against my foster parents' legs as they said their good-byes, mingling tears with snot as they dripped down the front of my pretty dress. I feared I would never see them again. I never did.

As my eyes focused on the old forsaken door, still lying on the ground, I thought that even new paint could not salve the ugliness that was creeping over my body.

From the day I was returned to my old family, I felt no different from the old rotten potatoes I scavenged from trash bins. My insides felt the same way the outside of the old house looked. It still had the broken door lying on the dirt in the driveway, broken beer bottles, and walls dirty with cobwebs. And the weeds. Everywhere, weeds. The weeds that never needed watering grew up along the neighbors' fences, around the house and porch, and up against the withering, scraggly fruit trees along the side of the yard. Everything looked like old junk. I felt like junk.

***

Now five, almost six years old, with long, blond, matted hair, feet without shoes, sporting tar and dirt like a widely dispersed birthmark, I recessed further into being a shy, anxious child. My anxiety was elevated by the loudness that reverberated so often within the walls of my dingy home.

Veronica and Howard's hate-filled relationship tormented all of us for two more years. I tried to close my ears to the words that would never be uttered in churches or in other children's homes.

Leaving my house at sun-up and returning after dark, I learned early how to take care of myself. Grandma worried about my gadabouts. She once asked me how I could tolerate the smell inside those dumpster bins. Glowing with pride, I showed her my latest find. With a shrug I said, "They're not so bad once you get used to them, Grandma." Compared to the fresh, close-up, in-your-face smell of the dog poop Howard smeared on me, trash bins smelled heavenly. Most of all, I wanted to avoid Howard and my mother as often as I could, especially their eyes—his foreboding, violent, or vacant, and hers angry, hate-filled, or blank. Those big old trash bins provided the perfect hiding place for a child that never felt safe.

I felt bitter hatred for Howard, but sometimes there were other feelings right alongside the bitter ones. I didn't understand just why, but there was some kind of softness in my heart each week when he brought home the milk bottles. It was the highest-valued commodity in our household, and was carefully rationed to each of us.

Watching him carry the heavy wire crate of glass milk bottles always brought feelings of surprised tenderness. Howard performed this task with military-like precision, week after week, year after year. Carrying the crate inside the house, he gently placed the container on the floor by the refrigerator. Kneeling down, as if the open fridge were his special holy altar, he would lift each bottle, wipe it off with a clean rag and stand and place it with painstaking exactness in a row on the top shelf. His kneeling and standing was like a genuflection, and he performed this task with inexplicable reverence. It was like he was conveying love and mercy to those bottles of milk that he wasn't able to extend to his family or to himself. With an observable sense of pride, he would close the refrigerator door and carefully wipe it clean. I always felt a strange sense of awe as I watched this ritual. On those occasions, when our eyes would meet, I felt as though he was thanking me for recognizing his intent. It wasn't much, but it was at least one job well done to support a family that never had enough food, love, or peace to go around.

Silver and Turquoise

MY MOTHER BEGAN dating Doc right after she separated from Howard, the dad with the choking hands. Doc had once been a practicing medical doctor in the San Diego area, but he hadn't worked since he surrendered to his daily drinking. Now living a subsistence life at the bottom of the economic scale, his home was an old, small trailer in a broken-down mobile home park.

Doc was an avid rock hound who loved going out in the desert areas in eastern Southern California. Next to smoking and drinking, he enjoyed collecting unusual rocks, mineral specimens, and, when lucky, gemstones.

He and my mother had a set of tools used for splitting and shaping rocks, which they kept rolled neatly in a deerskin cloth. I inherited these tools after my mother's death, and I shivered every time I saw them. Doc was also a shortwave radio fanatic. This was a popular hobby during the 1940s and 1950s for people who were keenly interested in news broadcasts from various locations around the world. Here Doc heard frequent UFO rumors, as the sightings and reports came so often in 1952. Doc also read science fiction magazines, which I remember seeing strewn all over the inside of his junky car. He paid no attention to the empty beer cans, candy wrappers, crunched-up cigarette packs, and dirty clothes, and there were always empty peanut butter jars in there, too, which seemed to be his mainstay.

Doc, just like Howard, was a drunk. The biggest difference was that Doc didn't get mean-tempered when he drank. He opened his first can of beer and popped a cigarette between his lips every morning the second his feet hit the floor. In those days, if one functioned, even if minimally, nobody thought they were an alcoholic. Doc and my mother had many good times hanging around together, and for a long time he was good to us kids.

Along with his .22 rifle, Doc would take Mom and us kids out for a day of shooting. Not really a day of shooting, it consisted of driving toward the mountains, stopping at a bar for a couple of hours of drinks, then proceeding to shoot a box of shells at tin cans. Then heading home, which included a stop at another bar for several more hours of drinking. We sat around, waiting impatiently, or sometimes played shuffleboard. No one had reason to imagine the impending danger.

I liked Doc, or maybe it was that I just liked his lack of intensity. The dad with the empty eyes carried a sense of foreboding, and I felt as if I were walking in a perpetual minefield every time I was in his presence. Doc's demeanor was calm and laid-back, and he patiently explained things like how to put up a tent or how his rock tools were used to cut and shape.

Often, my mother, brothers, and I went with Doc on camping trips near the ocean. He had an old camper and a big tent. We dug for clams and oysters, and set traps for lobsters. I would get upset when they boiled the lobsters in hot water; I felt sorry for them. Doc would try to force me to eat some, but I always threw it up. I still react that way today if I try to eat lobster. But other than that, Doc did nice things with us kids, which must have been a relief to our mother after separating from Howard's abuse.

Perhaps it was this feeling of trust with Doc that allowed my mother to send me on a ten-day vacation with him to New Mexico. I was excited to go anywhere in those days of innocence; I had already become quite the vagabond.

I overheard Doc and my mother talking about how anxious he was to get to New Mexico. He was aching to hear more detailed stories about UFOs. He was also excited about the gem and mineral show where we would camp. Early one summer morning, at the crack of dawn, Doc and I set off from San Diego pulling the old camper. I recall the endless ride across the hot, dusty desert. Wearing only my panties, I hung over the front seat while incessantly chattering at Doc with all of my seven-year-old enthusiasm. As events would progress, it would be last time that I relaxed enough around anyone to allow them to see me in my underwear.

Even with a cigarette dangling from his lips, Doc could still drive and hold a beer in his right hand. He steered with his left hand, while his left arm rested on the open door frame. For some reason, the cigarette smoke was comforting. I suppose it reminded me of my grandmother, who was rarely without a lit cigarette.

We finally arrived at our destination. I was breathless. My eyes and ears were taking in all the joyful sights and sounds of the carnival-type festivities. The various food smells were heavenly, and people shared willingly with one another. There was food in cups, food on plates, food on sticks, and all kinds of dips to stuff it all into. People spread colorful blankets everywhere for covering, sitting, and even just decorating. Among the craft tents, young and old alike were beading necklaces, bracelets, and earrings. Others were weaving things of beauty to wear or display. It was the colors that dazzled my child eyes more than what their hands were making. There were many displays of different types of rocks of all colors and shapes. I even saw fossils of dinosaurs and petrified trees. I had never seen so many *things* in one place.

But it was the depth of compassion in the eyes of the quiet Native American merchants that seemed to float into my soul—especially the eyes of the old women. I can close my eyes and recall the smells of sage and sweet-grass, and the sight of the many textures of silver, turquoise, and leather on display in open booths.

There was one old woman in particular whose eyes seemed to penetrate right into me with beams of warmth and wisdom. Her gaze somehow seemed to weave something protective around my spirit. I still feel that warmth when I think of her.

For several days, I had a glorious time. One night, a Native American tribe did a rain dance while dressed in their traditional clothes. Later that night it rained. I was so impacted by the power I believe emanated from that dance, that I think I became a believer in the strength of prayer and willful intention that very night.

Doc drank beer constantly, except when he was passed out. Toward the end of our stay, he seemed to get drunk and pass out more often. One night, as I lay in my twin bed in the tiny camper, he called to me.

He said, quite pleasantly at first, "Come and get into bed with me, Honey." I was an extremely affectionate child at that time, but remember feeling such foreboding in my stomach that I didn't want to answer him and pretended to be asleep. His beckoning became more intense each time that he called me, until finally, losing patience, he said, "God damn it, Dawn, I said get over here *now*." By the tone of his voice, I knew that I had to go or he would hurt me.

My feet were heavy with dread as I shuffled over and my stomach felt sick as I climbed into his stinky bed. He pulled me close against his damp, clammy skin. He took my hand and placed it on his penis. I tried not to breathe or move a single muscle in my body, hoping to avoid making the situation any more threatening.

From the father with the choking hands, I had learned how to play dead. So it was easy now to think myself dead. He said irritably, "Now squeeze." Frustrated with my feeble attempts, he angrily added, "No, not like that, like this," as he placed his hand over mine to make the rhythm to his liking. This repulsive act of touching him seemed to go on for hours, my seven-year-old body frozen into a twisted, ugly position. I imagined I was like the tumbleweeds that I had seen strewn across the desert floor and mashed up against fences on the drive to

New Mexico. My thoughts started to focus on the wet, slimy lobsters he had tried to make me eat when we were camping. I wanted to vomit, like then, but I knew if I vomited I would make things worse.

I don't recall how this episode ended, or if it was repeated. I do remember that when I was back in my bed, I curled up into a tight little ball to keep anything else from getting me. Hidden deep under the covers in the near one-hundred-degree temperature, eyes shut, I tried hard not to cry out loud.

Once he woke up and said in a menacing voice, "You better shut your mouth before I give you something to cry about."

I stuffed the corner of the sheet as far back in my mouth as it would go. Although gagging, I managed to remain silent. My pillow was soaked with tears and snot, but I didn't move. I was too scared to sleep the rest of the night.

At daybreak, I quickly dressed in my usual dirty pedal pushers and T-shirt, and snuck out the camper door. Few people were awake at the fair, so I wandered around in a dazed state for some time. Then I noticed her again, the old Indian woman sitting on her blanket, just like she was the last time I saw her. Her eyes called to me to come and sit by her. I sat on the very edge of her blanket facing in the same direction that she was facing. I was not yet ready for any eyes on me. She allowed me to sit quietly for several hours. Without a word or touch, she seemed to absorb enough of the trauma in my system to enable me to finally get up and slowly walk away. Just like that, I left with a new-found fire in my belly.

When Doc finally stumbled out of the camper, the sun was already high in the sky. I could tell by the menacing look on his face that he was in a foul mood. As soon as he set his eyes on me, I felt the fury coming.

He grabbed me by the arm and threatened to beat the stuffing out of me if I told our "secret." I thought back to my favorite doll, one that I had rescued from the dumpster. I remembered how terrible she looked with her stuffing hanging out. I knew my grandmother sewed the doll's insides back together with a needle and thread and part of an old, stained sheet, but I wasn't sure if I could be sewed back together again if my stuffings were beaten out of me.

I hugged the door handle of the car on the long, hot, dusty trip home without ever speaking a word. I focused my eyes on the tumbleweeds blowing around the sandy desert floor and bouncing over rocks. With each passing mile, I grew to hate tumbleweeds with every speck of my being. I remembered back to the time I was running across a field during a sandstorm when a tumbleweed bush plastered its prickly bristles against me, sticking me, hurting me. Glaring out from the car window, I put my fierce hatred on them.

For the entire ride home to California I steadfastly refused his constant offerings of ice cream and wouldn't respond to any conversation. Looking back, that was quite a feat of rebellion for a seven-year-old.

Never the same after that trip, I felt that I could trust no one. I felt as dirty on the inside as the neighbors could see I was on the outside. I didn't care much about running fast anymore, nor for the sweet pea hugs inside my mouth. Even my beloved brother's beautiful smile had little meaning or satisfaction now. I felt dirty—dirty outside, dirty inside, dirty, dirty, dirty. I felt suffocated beneath all of the dirt. I desperately wanted to sleep. Just sleep.

Beneath the sanctuary of the Jesus, Mary, and Joseph statues, I whispered my ordeal to grandmother. With eyes of terror, she listened to my tale, hanging her head in sadness. The only thing she ever said was, "Oh, sweet Jesus. Oh, sweet Jesus." Sprinkling holy water over me again and again didn't make me feel clean the way I felt when she washed my tattered dolls. In fact, inexplicably, it added another layer to my feelings of dirt. Grandma just wasn't able to say what I needed to hear—that it wasn't my fault. I assume Grandma told my mother, because I never had to see Doc again. The incident was apparently forgotten by everyone but me.

Ragdoll Tarnished

SANDWICHED BETWEEN TELEVISION shows touting moral values, such as *Ozzie and Harriet* and *Father Knows Best*, were coffee tables acceptably littered with girly magazines like *Playboy Magazine*. So it seems odd to me that the 1950s is still considered to epitomize the generation of the ideal family, when just beneath the "happy family" façade was often an atmosphere of violence, terror, and alcoholism. We'll never know to what extent this occurred, since women who reported it in those days were thought to merely be having sexual fantasies. "Experts" discounted stories of incest, giving it a one-in-a-million probability. Battered women were often thought to have provoked their husband into abusing them.

I don't recall the exact sequence of events, or which man came first, but for a while I allowed myself to be passed around the neighborhood like a sexual rag doll in exchange for cookies and candy.

One of these men was the kind, old, Presbyterian minister who everyone loved because of all of the good he did in the neighborhood. By all appearances, he seemed like a trustworthy man of the cloth. He didn't scare or hurt me, like some men had; he only required that I stand still while he placed his hand down my panties. First, he slowly and ritualistically unwrapped two chocolate bars, placing them in each of my hands while saying a prayer. Hungry as usual, and with candy being a rare treat, I was more than content with the exchange. The minister rubbed me while touching himself with his other hand, and made little sounds like dogs growling. I disconnected my mind by eating my candy bars and dreaming about rollerskating. I would just let the top half of my body and the bottom half remain disconnected. Besides, by now this kind of touching was beginning to feel good because I was linking the actions with a reward.

Mr. and Mrs. Kelly, an elderly couple, lived two doors away from us. Mrs. Kelly was always kind to me. She freely offered fruit from her trees and fresh-baked peanut butter cookies with a glass of lemonade. Unlike my home, theirs was sunny, clean, and smelled like lavender soap. I was delighted to even set foot in their home, because no other neighbor ever invited me in. Mrs. Kelly even allowed me to sit on their furniture, albeit while it was covered in plastic. Mr. Kelly would show me his coin collection and give me long hugs. I didn't like the hugging part; somehow it always felt creepy, though I didn't know why.

Mrs. Kelly came home earlier than expected one day to find her husband touching me. The whole neighborhood could hear her shrill screams through those thin Army barracks walls: "You little bastard, and after all those cookies I baked for you! Get out of my house, you little slut!" I didn't know what the word "slut" meant, but I knew it must be bad. I knew that I was doing something bad. I really didn't want Mr. Kelly's old creepy hands on me, yet I couldn't resist the banquet of homemade cookies. Relieving my hunger in exchange for touching was a trade-off that I was fast learning. It seemed fair somehow to me—like goods exchanged for services rendered. Running down the street as other children watched, I could tell they knew I had been doing something wrong. I didn't know which would be harder now— not eating Mrs. Kelly's cookies when I was so hungry, or eating her words of condemnation.

I had thought that it was the house without paint, the naked feet, the dirty blond hair, and the trash bin smell that clung to my ragged pedal pushers that caused the neighbors to reject me. But now added to my reasons for rejection was the lingering sound of a neighbor's wife shrieking names at me. "Bastard! Bastard!" What does *that* mean, I pondered. Where had I heard that word before?

***

"Never you mind," I said to myself as I continued my trash bin scavenging. I took pride in my ability to sort through and select the most desirable discarded fruit and vegetables to contribute to our family's next meal. It helped that my grandmother never failed to praise my efforts. Increasingly, I felt a gnawing urgency to rescue the most filthy and broken discarded dolls from the bellies of the smelly trash bins. I cleaned them and held them as close as possible, as if I alone could keep them safe.

Due to her severe ulcers, my grandmother could only eat soft foods like cottage cheese or baby food from jars. Sometimes, in the middle of the night, I would sneak a few bites of the baby food that was forbidden to me. Returning to bed, I'd burn with the shame of stealing my grandmother's meager fare. I repeatedly vowed to God to only take food from the dumpsters, but mimicking the broken promises of every addict with an obsession, the thief in me would lie in wait for another opportunity to steal more of my grandmother's pittance.

***

Peeking out from under the covers as Grandma stood over me, I protested in vain as she sprinkled me with a few drops of her precious cache of holy water. She'd done this every night for as long as I could remember. She was certain that the holy water had special powers to keep evil away from me. When I was willing to listen, she was more than willing to remind me of Saint Teresa of Avila, who had so loved the consecrated mystery of holy water.

After sprinkling me to ward off evil influences, she would sometimes light another cigarette and sit beside me while I fell asleep, which I always pretended to do. Then she would begin the ritual that meant so much to my child's heart, which I peeked out of the covers to watch. First, she opened her Bible and read a few verses by the light of her Lady of Fatima night-light. Next, she pulled the tight rubber band from her bun and allowed her hair to fall along her weary neck. Standing erect, she relaxed her shoulders, marked with indents from her 32-DDD bra. That was a lot of bosom for someone who stood no taller than five feet on her tip-toes, but to me she was perfect: she was my *grand*mother.

Against the wall was her sacred altar, and behind it, the large crucifix that hung directly above Mother Mary's head. Now raising her arms wide as she faced her shrine, she began her silent prayers. I stayed silent, but wondered if she, or even God, could hear my breath beneath my sheet.

She remained in that precise position for what seemed like an eternity, until I found myself drifting off to sleep. As I rolled over, the last thing I saw was her shadow on the wall, enveloping me in a sense of the sacred. Not that I understood what sacred meant, but I had the feeling of being peacefully sheltered by some power that was capable of mysterious and wonderful things.

***

As she stitched together my latest rescued doll, she began to tell me the story I had heard so many times before. From the soft look in her hazel-colored eyes, I understood that the recitation itself imparted a sense of peace to her. Our tiny bedroom held such a serene feeling of calm when she was about to retell this story. Sitting cross-legged on my bed, holding one of my many repaired dolls, I gently rocked us. Barely restraining my anticipation, I urged my grandmother to begin.

"When I was a little girl like you, Dawnie, living in the orphanage, Sister Veronica would tell us the story of old Brother Lawrence, the shyest monk in the monastery. Most everyone thought he was just plain stupid. Even the other priests thought him dumb because no matter how difficult or dirty were the chores they gave him, he would always do them with a cheerful face."

As always, I stopped my grandma and asked the same question, and, as always, she waited just a moment for me to remember before she answered. "Grandma, why did Brother Lawrence do that? Why would he always be happy, no matter what?"

"Well, Dawnie," she said, "It was because he decided early in his life to do everything placed before him as if he were doing it for Jesus himself. When he fried an egg, he would tell himself that he was frying it for Jesus and wanted it to be perfect. Every pan that he washed, he washed for Jesus. In this way of remembering his love of Jesus, Brother Lawrence was able to tolerate anything life brought his way."

And then she ended as she always did, "Don't forget, Dawnie, to always keep something with you to help you remember your Father in Heaven. It is not the *thing* itself that's important; it's the *always remembering* that matters."

I knew that was why I never saw my grandmother without her rosary beads either in her hands or softly tucked away in her big, five pocket apron, right next to her hanky and cigarettes.

I found great comfort in my grandmother's stories of her beloved God. I recognized and respected her efforts to model her spirituality after her Saint Teresa of Avila or old Brother Lawrence—enduring all the hardships in *her* life for the love of her Jesus. Maybe it was because she demonstrated that kind of faith without demanding the same from others that I have come to believe so deeply in the goodness of life. I have modeled my own love for the Eternal from her daily devotions. I often recall her most memorable words to me: "Dawnie, Dawnie, it does not matter *how* you believe as long as you *do* believe."

As a young child I was learning a deep and abiding love for this mysterious God of my grandmother's. I began to see something *other-worldly* in the arms of the sweet peas, the eucalyptus trees, my dog's kisses, the welcoming swayed back of the old horse, Dolly, life breathed into my tattered dolls by my grandmother's gnarled fingers, and even in the coal-black eyes of my dad who carried in the heavy milk crates.

***

My mother, however, found Grandma's definition of everything as being God's holy will to be yet another justification for her own bitterness. As far as she was concerned, Grandma's refusal to deal realistically with the hardships placed before her was a sign of a delusional mind. My mother would often yell sarcastically at my grandmother, "If the damned house caught on fire, you'd be more likely sit in the middle of it and pray than call the fire department!"

As a child I couldn't understand just how hollow and even hurtful my grandmother's biblical chides sounded to my mother. But Grandma stayed true to herself and her faith, even as her grandchildren cried with hunger or the electricity was turned off because of an unpaid bill. By necessity, my mother became the head of the household. She became the financial manager, the disciplinarian, and decision-maker. She must have felt very lonely shouldering all the decisions and problems.

Meanwhile, my brother and I, our grandmother, some neighbors, and even our local parish priest, dismissed our mother as being all but the antichrist due to her lack of trust in God. Anything my mother did or said in resistance to our grandmother's wishes was viewed by my brother and me as being mean and selfish. We saw Grandma as the consummate saint and our mother as the consummate sinner. To us she was always "missing the mark" like Thomas had in doubting Jesus.

Well into our adulthood, my older brother and I saw our mother as mean, cruel, and petty, while remembering our grandmother as sweet, meek, and loving. We blamed our mother for the way Grandma slinked around the house, acting like a victim to our mother's mean tongue. Today, I can only imagine that my grandmother's passive-aggressive behavior must have been what incited at least part of my mother's perpetual anger. After all, who can ever defend themselves against the "righteous?" And who can defend the "irreligious?"

Once, during a holiday season, my grandmother tried to talk my mother into having a homeless couple over for Christmas dinner, despite the fact that the only food we would have would be what was brought to us in a Salvation Army basket. Sometimes, when we were chosen, we would receive a fresh turkey from some business that donated food.

"Veronica," Grandma began in a sweet, cajoling tone of voice, "On Sunday after mass, Father Mulligan said that the Allen's don't got any food for Christmas dinner. I was kind of thinking maybe we could have them over and share ours with them."

Mother's voice sounded like she was talking to a child as she spoke with the same weary impatience she always used on me, "Mother, you know we're only going to have enough food for our own family." She paused and then continued, "Besides that, there's no room for them to sit."

My grandmother's voice became even calmer, anchored as it was in her certainty that she was defending the Lord's own place at our table. "Now you know, Veronica, that I'll just eat my usual cottage cheese and you can give them my part of the food basket." Without hesitation, she began to quote the Bible: "If a man shuts his ears to the cry of the poor, he too will cry out and not be answered."

"For Christ sake, Mother, we *are* the poor." Without pausing for a breath, my mother yelled at me, "Dawn, stop biting your damn fingernails."

Please, Jesus, Just Let Me Die

PEERING DOWN FROM the rugged granite mountain ridges some twenty miles north of the Mexican border and seventeen miles east of the Pacific Ocean, one can only guess at the breathlessness of the early mission padres seeing the basin below. They named the valley El Cajon. The name means "the big box" because that is how the flat valley floor seemed. The eventual agrarian heartland would prove a perfect support for citrus, avocados, grapes and barley. It was near these foothills that I learned to love solitude and an old horse named Dolly, and to devour mounds of mashed potatoes. It was also where I learned to hate tumbleweeds, tarantulas, and the effects of alcohol.

The family composition shifted when I turned seven and my big brother was eleven. Mother, hospitalized for several weeks with complications from jaundice, followed by months of bed rest, presented the opportunity for Howard to find himself a new woman. Even before the divorce papers were filed, he was gone.

So the father with the alcohol smell and piercing eyes moved to an even louder dwelling with more strife than he had bargained for. For some inexplicable reason, even knowing how abusive Howard was to my younger brother, Russell, and to me, our mother continued to send us to his place on weekends. As an adult, I presume that her choice had something to do with child support payments. As a child, I was just plain scared.

Vi, our new stepmother, was a tall, obese woman with hair the feel and color of straw. She could drink booze with the best of them. Her bulbous nose displayed little veins popping out on the sides that looked like a road map. She smelled of beer, a smell that combined sickeningly with the kind of cheap perfume I had often whiffed at the five-and-ten-cent store. Every time Vi laid her glassy eyes on me, I felt like she wanted to eat me for dessert. She was huge, clumsy, and, in some ways, hurtful towards me. Whenever she touched me, my body became rigid and my face scrunched up. When she would grab me and pull me into her massive bosom for a hug, I would hold my breath and count numbers—one more trick I had learned to use in situations that were difficult. I knew that she delighted in having me around, but her habitual drunkenness made her delight feel oppressive, and even scary. I couldn't trust what she might do.

At the same time, I felt her kindness and desire to please me. Vi lovingly made my favorite food, mashed potatoes with mounds of butter on top. The mixed feelings I experienced toward her added to my confusion toward adults in general. It seemed impossible to make sense out of their behavior. I overwhelmingly preferred solitude, a trait deeply embedded in me to this day and only overcome with effort.

For a while, Howard co-habitated contentedly with his new wife and her near-adult, parasitic sons. I hated my new stepbrothers, who were in their late teens. Their lives centered on continuous beer consumption. The dilapidated trailer, with its taped up windows, reeked like a sleazy tavern, forever forming a mental image of what "trailer trash" would be.

Hiding from my drunken teenage brothers was always a challenge. Their messianic goal was to drag me around by my hair and grab my body parts every time I came into view. My goal was to avoid them at all costs. They were cruel young men who spent enormous amounts of time incarcerated for crimes that I never understood.

Years later, I asked my younger brother, Russell, if he remembered any of this. He said, "Oh yes, Baby Girl, I remember the times I would hear you screaming while you were locked in the bathroom with one of those monsters while the other beat on me. I would stand outside the bathroom and pound on the door. When I'd run to get Vi, she laughed. She'd say, 'Oh, Honey, they're only playing. Now you just run along.' I knew by your screams that *you* were not just playing. I hated knowing that I couldn't help you."

Amazingly, during this time, Howard stopped hurting me; in fact, he totally ignored me. (I would one day learn that he tried to "unadopt" Ronnie and me, but the courts wouldn't grant his petition.)

The only thing that made those weekend visits to my dad's bearable was a neighbor's filthy old horse named Dolly. I thought her to be very sad, and she was horribly swaybacked, but somehow we understood each other intimately. Dolly allowed me to climb up onto her weary, old, bare back, where I would slide down to the lowest part to feel cradled. She and I, ever so slowly, would walk way out into the big pasture, where we would daydream our way through the day. Sometimes I would cry into her matted mane while she nuzzled my neck. I always brought Dolly any carrots I could find when scavenging in the dumpsters. Like the big old eucalyptus trees and broken dolls I befriended, Dolly never cared about my filthy feet or matted hair. We became good friends over the three years I was forced to go to that wretched trailer.

Everyone but Vi laughed at my tears when I was told that the old mare had died from starvation. To console me, Vi made me my very own bowl of mashed potatoes my favorite way, with butter stacked on top. Later I could realize what a kind stepmother she really was—most of the time.

I was glad that my Ronnie was not forced into the weekend visits: he would have tried to protect me, and being older, stronger, and violent, my stepbrothers would have seriously hurt him. He never had to witness the deafening mayhem that precipitated incredible violence between Howard, Vi, and my stepbrothers—airborne pans and pieces of fried chicken flung at one another in heated warfare. The frequency with which this occurred made it seem like some kind of demented family ritual. By the time the food was put on the table, it was difficult to imagine the intended menu. I could only guess by the color of the mess on the plates, piled with food off of the floor. Being in a state of perpetual hunger, this never bothered me—besides, the food was still better than what I didn't have at home.

As difficult and frightening as these peculiar afternoon rituals were to me, they ultimately served to calm the family atmosphere, sort of like a pressure cooker that has blown its top and has no steam left. Afterwards, the family squeezed around the card table, eating supper as if nothing out of the ordinary had just occurred. My insides felt like scattered alphabet letters. However desperate I was to put my parts back into some order, I just couldn't figure which way they went.

It Was a Great Fire

SUMMER, 1952. Hot, dry, and windy. Tumbleweeds blew everywhere. I obsessed about them. I hated them. They were the reason my life was ugly. That I was ugly. The tinder-dry conditions of a vacant field filled with tumbleweeds was perfect for my plan. Just one match from the small matchbook hidden inside the back pocket of my scruffy navy blue pedal pushers, coupled with my seven-year-old rage—rage that was large enough for another Hiroshima—was all that was needed to eliminate the tumbleweeds, the source of my pain. I was sure of it.

Tension had eased a bit now that the dad with black eyes was gone from our house, but Mother's depression was scary. I tried to focus on my brother's dimples, Grandma's prayers, sweet peas, trees and Zany.

Zany was my brother Ronnie's dog, but Ronnie shared everything with me—from his beloved dog to the best pieces of bread (he would actually eat the crust and save the soft inside part for me).

How can one possibly describe a child's love for a dog? I was seven when Zany, a long-haired Collie puppy, became part of our family. He was smart as a whip and fiercely protective of children, and our family loved him. I spent countless hours not only playing with Zany, but crying into his soft fur. One time while I was babysitting four young children, the eighteen-month-old boy ran into the street. Zany ran after him, pulled him down by his diaper, and sat on him, barking wildly, until I could get there. A human mother could not have offered more love and comfort than Zany as he tenderly licked away my tears.

Over the years, I tried to tell my grandmother of my anger, but she always shushed me, fearing that we would be heard beyond our walls and get in trouble. "I'm already in trouble, Grandma," I wanted to say. If I had known how to take my own life, I would have. I wanted to scream with my whole body. Instead, I picked at myself, gouging and tearing the skin on my arms. Grandma prayed to her God—the God that didn't stop the abuse.

Memories of the trip to New Mexico with my mother's boyfriend haunted me. Dodging my stepbrothers on weekends, facing relentless drunken warfare between my stepparents, and the neighborhood men groping, probing, always probing, became too much for me. My stammering and pants-wetting increased. I thought no one would notice if I could just dry my panties with old newspapers from the dumpsters. I either couldn't smell the lingering, pungent odor, or I was just used to my own smell.

And then there was school. The weight of dread stooped my shoulders as I approached the steps of my Catholic classroom. Sister RoseIleana was almost as terrifying as my dad. She carried a large yardstick, sometimes whacking children without provocation. At that time, it was a sin to be left-handed. A sin worthy of daily ruler whacks that turned my left hand red and sore and flooded my body with shame. I knew that something at the very core of me was evil. I deserved to be hit. They said so. They hit. I accepted.

Eventually, I learned to use my right hand. Not very well, I might add, and I couldn't grasp letters or numbers. To atone for my sins, the nuns placed adhesive tape over my mouth and made me stand in front of the older children for what seemed like hours. Thinking of ways to die helped me get through. That, and counting. I always counted. Eventually, I was fitted with glasses, the apparent remedy in those days for any child that had difficulty reading letters and numbers. Except the glasses did nothing to help my comprehension. The kids laughed when I stuttered, or maybe it was the smell of pee that made them laugh. Defiantly, one day I fed my glasses to She-She, my favorite dumpster.

Every Friday I had to confess my sins to the priest. I can't say which terrified me more: the darkness of the tiny confessional box, or the priest hidden behind the little black window inside of the cramped box. I knew I was a sinner because I used the wrong hand, I argued with my brother, and I would sneak food to eat when I was supposed to fast before communion. I begged God to help me, to make me good. Silence.

What does a seven-year-old child do with boundless rage? Set fire to a large, parched, vacant grass field, of course; the hottest, loudest, and fastest fire possible. Unfortunately, the death-defying intensity of the flames could not begin to match my internal rage. I started the fire *at* them, at *all* of them. Those who were hurting me along with those who couldn't or wouldn't stop the ones who were hurting me—I hated them, I hated them all! When the firefighters came to my house and asked why, I said that the sun must have accidentally ignited the matches. With head bowed, I murmured my apologies. Strangely, my mother did not punish me for this act. Everyone was incredulous that I could have done something so outrageous, since—at least, in their thinking—I had otherwise always been a shy, quiet, and obedient child.

But secretly, I was glad I had killed the tumbleweeds.

A New Me but for the Chickens

ON JULY 4, 1955, the New York Yankees lost to the Boston Red Sox seven to four. Marilyn Monroe graced the front page of *Tempo* magazine, which could be purchased for fifteen cents. Marilyn's bathing suit was labeled with the words, "Beware of Danger."

It would be seven years before I would have any reason to pay attention to any of these happenings. The day of spectacular fireworks and bodacious flag flying was also my tenth birthday, and we were moving to a new house in a brand new neighborhood, not one of those converted barracks.

I was enlivened with the prospect of a new start, a new life away from the house without grass and the accusing eyes of the neighbors who knew of the shame within the house with no paint. I can recall with great accuracy the desire to recreate myself, to make a new me to match the new neighborhood. I thought and thought about who I could become and how to go about creating an acceptable me. I wanted people to smile when they saw me instead of withering their faces up like a prune.

The event that began to ease the tight bands around my growing young heart was the stranger that my mother brought home one night when I was ten. Donald was his name, and she announced without ceremony that he was now our new dad. A young man in his twenties, fresh out of the Navy, he had snappy brown eyes that seemed to dance with gold sparkles when he laughed.

We would soon learn that he laughed often and loud. So loud, in fact, that my grandmother said that he could wake up the dead. Grandmother had many odd sayings like "wake up the dead." We grew to like Donald's loudness, which was fun-filled and kind. Also, this new dad loved children—probably because, at only twenty-three, he himself was a like a big kid.

He often took me with him on his dry-cleaning route, and always managed to get me an ice cream treat without asking for anything in return. He frequently took my older brother and me to the mountains to shoot tin cans. This new dad could never understand why I was so intent on shooting the tumbleweeds, and he never learned of my shameful time with Doc.

It was he who moved us to our lovely new home. I grew to love and trust my new dad.

So now, with all of my ten-year-old imagination and savvy, I pondered ways to remake myself. One day I watched with envy as a group of Blue Birds and Girl Scouts loaded onto a bus for a field trip. I felt that familiar pain way deep inside that seemed to say, "Only clean girls can wear uniforms." But seeing those girls also gave me a great idea. I recalled that Girl Scouts of America had a motto about doing good deeds and that Blue Birds touted something about "being a helper at home, school, and neighborhood."

"That's it, that's it!" I exclaimed to myself. I would become a good, kind, and helpful girl to my neighbors. The street name of our new home was Silvery Lane. All of the homes on our long, curved street nestled up to the hill behind us, had lawns and flowers, and truly seemed silvery in reflected sunlight. I thought that the houses themselves stood proud and showed no signs of obvious neglect or shame.

My remake plan seemed to be working; when I walked around the neighborhood people smiled and actually stopped and talked with me. I made friends with a girl named Mary who lived down the street. Her family liked me a lot because they found me to be polite and helpful. They also thought I could possibly become a positive influence on their contrary daughter. They began taking me on all kinds of wonderful family outings. I had great adventures, despite the fact that Mary's father was a late-stage alcoholic. It is truly a miracle that we all survived his driving and the way he flew his private plane. He literally went from bar to bar, by plane, boat, or car, with his wife and us four kids in tow.

Two years after we moved to Silvery Lane, I had accomplished my goal of reinventing myself. Neighbors' faces lit up when they saw me. I was welcomed into their homes, and had come a long way out of the shell of shyness hell. By age twelve, I was standing tall and full of hope.

And then came the chickens. There were hundreds of them placed right in our backyard. Without a coop. Dirty, smelly, noisy, bloody chickens. My mother and Don decided that chickens would be a great way to supplement our food supply. We children were required to catch them, kill them, cut off their heads, clean, and eat them. I *never* participated. The chickens scared me, embarrassed me, and their very presence tormented me. However, even though I despised their filthy presence, I could not stand to see them killed. For my disobedience, I was constantly sent to bed without supper, which was just fine with me.

I learned that the tenuousness of relationships, connections, and reputations could be turned upside down in a single day by any number of outside possibilities. Overnight, neighbors' smiles disappeared, doors closed on me, and my bare feet were no longer welcomed under the tables of my formerly hospitable neighbors. I was now met with the old, familiar, pinched-like-a-prune expression that broke my heart; all the neighbors wanted to talk about were "the goddamn chickens."

***

Disheartened by the rejection, I determined to learn about people's wants, needs, and desires. I devoted myself to the study of people's faces, body language, and tone of voice with the tenacity of a marathon runner. I studied expressed and unexpressed desires. I thought I could learn the secret to making people accept me by fulfilling their "missings." For example, years later I had a neighbor whose son always failed to remember her on mother's day. This was especially painful because she had lost her only other child, a daughter. Hearing this "missing," I started sending her mother's day cards, and I have not missed one in twenty years.

Though it may sound thoughtful, it is an arduous task to center one's personal maturation around observing and attending to others with such intensity. The hypervigilance involved left me feeling outside of myself, always scanning the atmosphere for what it was that I thought I needed to fill in or complete for people. Not that I could do such a thing in actuality, but, by God, I tried. All that, just to be accepted.

I could never have imagined that I would create a facet of my character that would become phony, placating, and accommodating just to be accepted. Just to fit in. Just to see a smile on someone's face when they saw me coming.

I believe now that that long-ago, deliberate decision was the basis for the recent comment of a good friend and colleague, Dean, who said, "Dawn, somewhere along the way, you learned to be an exquisite mirror of people's feelings or internal reality, but you are deceitful in that this way of relating comes from a *part* or *aspect* of yourself versus your *true self*." He was referring to what a 1970s human potential course, EST, would have called my "winning formula." I believe his observation is accurate.

The profound aspiration of my ten-year-old self became a pivotal conversion to the fundamental makeup of my projected persona. The positive aspect of this trait has been an ability to draw people to myself, which has been tremendously rewarding. The negative aspect is that I often appear more emotionally available than I am actually capable ofbeing. This discordant aspect of my character can cause great distress in my close relationships, hence Dean's comment about deceitfulness.

***

Fast-forward seven years from my physical relocation and recreation of self on Silvery Lane to the arrival of my shining prince. Within one week, he fell in love with the face that I presented to the world; however, he had his own agenda. He wanted to turn my guise into the appearance that he had idealized. Joey had long had a crush on Marilyn, who also created a magnificent persona—one formed out of a part of her original, Norma Jeane self. He worked hard to recreate my appearance to match her groomed presentation. I wish that he and I could have been forewarned of the impending danger. Perhaps then our two-year marriage would not have ended in such mutual devastation.

> "My work is the only ground I've ever had to stand on.
> I seem to have a whole superstructure with no foundation—but I'm working on the foundation."
>
> —Marilyn.

When you merely gold-plate something, it only gives it a thin covering, which eventually wears away; the underlying structure always surfaces. Without substance, it is only a façade.

Can Mice Climb, Ronnie?

THE WHOLE FAMILY seemed excited to sell the house that had become the chicken refuge. Mother and Don were opening a new dry-cleaning store in Ramona, California. Their spirits were high; they looked forward to a new adventure. I was grateful to escape the noisy, smelly, poop-ridden chickens and the neighbors' disgust.

Our family of six and our lovely collie, Zany, moved into a small, two-bedroom house in Ramona. We all seemed to adjust fairly well until Don met Richard at a local bar while Don was "just having a few beers," one of his newly discovered favorite pastimes.

Our lives would be changed forever by Richard, a charming but devious man who completely took over our lives.

Richard had four children under the age of ten and a very sick wife. They were without money or a place to live, and we took them in. Being a grown up thirteen-year-old, I stayed home from school for six weeks to take care of the four children while Richard's wife, Maria, was hospitalized.

The little house was so crowded that my brother, now seventeen, and I were relegated to sleeping on cots in the half-finished garage. What I most remember about that period, however, was the sound of the mice running around. Petrified, every night I asked my brother if the mice could climb up in our cots. He always replied, "No way, Honey, now you just go to sleep."

I believed him. I drifted off to sleep despite the sound of their little, scurrying feet. I think I would have come apart at the seams with fear had he not been there to comfort me.

My brother avoided the insane chaos by abruptly leaving home to join the Marines, just like his father before him. He grew into a man of honor but at the time I was anguished when he left and didn't say good-bye. My heart ached from missing him, just as it had when I was sent to the foster care home at age four.

After Mother and Don took Richard into their business, he promptly embezzled several thousand dollars—big money in those days—which resulted in bankruptcy. My mother maintained that my stepdad's bad judgment in befriending Richard forced her to leave him. But I clearly remember seeing my mother in the arms of charming Richard, and they were kissing.

Whatever the full reason for the breakup, I missed Don and regretted not having the chance to whisper a brief goodbye. Mother went to her grave never telling Don that she had officially divorced him. Her refusal to tell him was his punishment for the "sin" of bringing Richard home.

Everything happened so fast. In the span of one week, Richard and his family were gone. Don left forever, and my brother escaped into the night. Years later, Ronnie explained that he could not have witnessed the heartache his leaving would cause me.

Soon after, I sat on the sidewalk, watching in sadness, as the movers repossessed my mother's cherished furniture. I knew how hard she had worked to pay the finance company for that turquoise sectional couch. With the gold and black threads running every which way, I thought it to be the ugliest couch I ever saw. Nevertheless, it was *her* couch. What was left of my shattered heart broke further that morning when I saw her ashen face watch helplessly. In some mysterious way, the movers repossessed my mother's soul as well, because she was never the same afterward. She now had holes deeply embedded in her core. She had lost her father when she was ten, then *my* father, the love of her life. Three husbands gone, along with her business; lost were hopes of financial security, and vanished was her future. Even I understood that it wasn't about the furniture. It was about all of the thwarted dreams disappearing with the removal of each piece.

***

A few weeks later, my grandmother, mother, younger brother, and I moved from Ramona to National City, close to the Mexican border. Surprisingly, my mother had one more romantic relationship left in her. This time her lover was a late-stage alcoholic named Bill. His gravelly voice, alcoholic breath, and staggering gait invaded our lives for the next two years. A nice enough guy, but his glassed-over eyes, repetitive, stupid jokes, affectionate hugs, and unpredictable behavior were exhausting to be around. Unpredictable people still frighten me. Drunks are unpredictable.

After their breakup, we moved around the San Diego area like vagabonds several more times. Mother sank into a deep depression, surrendered to welfare, and quietly slid into the comforting arms of Valium.

Who's Sorry Now?

WHILE SITTING ON our twin beds, sharing a cigarette beneath Grandma's beloved statues of Jesus, Mary, and Joseph, Grandma and I practiced blowing smoke rings. We had gotten so good at this game that sometimes we could blow them right through each other's ring. We giggled like schoolgirls when that happened.

I would ask her, for the hundredth time, to tell me about my real father. What else better to do when your grandma is in a best-friend kind of mood than ask her to let you in on another girl-to-girl secret?

In the past, she had always shied away from the subject of my father's identity as if she feared my mother would walk in and somehow smell her disloyalty. But this day, with a sigh that seemed to reach all the way to her toes, Grandma stared off into space while slowly blowing the most perfect smoke ring ever, without even noticing she had done it. Looking up toward the ceiling with a faraway expression on her face, Grandma told me the story that I so longed for.

"Your father's name was Roland, and he was quite the handsome lad." Then Grandma's face seemed to grow soft, and it sort of glowed. It seemed to make her younger just to think about the days before my mother climbed inside herself and locked us all out of her soul. Looking at me for just a moment and then quickly away (as if looking at me would bring back the loss of those better times), she continued with the words I longed to hear more than any others: "Roland and your mother were wildly in love, Dawnie."

Now that I was almost fourteen, I guess Grandma thought I was old enough to talk to about such things. I mean, after all, she had been sharing her cigarettes with me for two years now. As she continued to recall the events of long ago, the faraway look returned to her face, but the softness was fading. I cringed inside; I knew that look. She got it whenever she was talking about hard things from the past. I thought, had the love between my parents faded *that* fast? I tried to stay very still; I didn't want her to stop.

"Roland thought your mother was the most beautiful woman he ever saw. He told me that more than once. He said he 'specially loved her skin. One time he told me that he thought she was as delicate as fine bone china. Every time your mother would come into the room where we were, he'd whisper to me, 'Doesn't she just remind you of an angel gliding in?' You know how she's always been about posture and all,

Dawnie. How she makes you stand up straight and makes you walk around with a book on your head? And how she yells at you to hold in your tummy?"

I momentarily turned my eyes from her face to stare at the glow emanating from the Lady of Fatima night-light on the altar—a soothing light with two children sitting at the figurine's feet. I had always found this night-light comforting.

I tried to keep my grandmother from noticing how red my face was as I recalled some of those things my mother said. "Men don't like girls with their stomachs sticking out," or, "It's much easier to catch flies with honey—learn to be sweet for men, Dawn." It was always about how to be and do in order to ensnare a man. In my mother's world, a woman was nothing without a man.

I slowed down my breathing to control my rising anger. I let my mind dwell on the air going in and out as I focused my eyes on the changing shapes of our collective smoke rings.

Grandma didn't really notice me now; she had moved into a semi-trance. She talked with a remembered pride in her eyes when recalling these stories of her daughter, totally oblivious to the fact that I was drowning in anger.

For so long I had ached for my mother's attention, but not in this way. This way just felt mean. Only yesterday she had said, "You used to look like a graceful racehorse, Dawn, but now that you got your body, you look like a goddamn plow horse." I didn't know what a plow horse looked like, but I remembered Dolly, the old swaybacked horse. She was filthy and pitiful, and God, I didn't want to look as ugly as Dolly. Turning my attention back to Grandma, I said, "Then what?"

"Anyways, Roland always said about how your mother danced with the lightness of an angel's wings. He was blushing when he said it, don't you know. He even said to me that her sea-blue eyes made his insides have feelings that only a woman can give a man. He was truly sweet on your mother, Dawnie."

He also told my grandmother that it was my mother's hands that most mesmerized him. Her long, delicate, china-like fingers moved with an innate elegance that captivated his eyes. She was even chosen by a modeling agency to model jewelry for the most expensive stores in New York City.

I wasn't surprised that Roland confided in Grandma. All the boys confided in her. Being such a homebody, she was always available, easy to talk to, and incredibly non-judgmental. And she knew her sports, especially baseball.

She knew everything there was to know about baseball. She knew the history of every team that ever played. But her love affair was with the New York Yankees. She loved that team almost as much as she loved her bible. My guy friends and their friends loved to sit and smoke cigarettes with my grandma while mulling over batting averages. I would come home to find all sorts of my guy friends laughing with my grandmother, and often my mother. I did my best to smile, but I resented that I had no privacy with *my* friends. I kept wondering why they didn't get their own friends (besides the disgusting June White, who let her husband have their own daughter for pleasure). But now I'm getting ahead of my own story.

Lighting another cigarette after handing the first lit one to me, Grandma continued, "But as much as he loved her, her poor grammar got on his nerves real bad. He knowed that he could never bring her home to meet his prim and proper mother, a stiff-skirt schoolteacher type, don't you know. Roland himself understood the desperate family situation your mother growed up in, causing the end of her education at grade eight—although, that was five grades more than I ever done. Even so, he was accepting of your mother the way she was."

When I needed a break from Grandma's storytelling, I concentrated on blowing the perfect smoke ring, but they never looked as good as Grandma's, nor could I suck the smoke up through my nostrils like she could. Even so, the smoke ring ritual gave me a way to manage all of the mixed up feelings swirling around in my tummy.

Part of these feelings wasn't just from hearing this story, but because Grandma suddenly started having one of her coughing spells, which usually caused a severe asthma attack. This happened frequently, especially when she was thinking about something that hurt her. With her bad heart condition, I was terrified she would cough herself to death right on the spot. I was also convinced that I'd die if I had to live in that family without her by my side. Holding my breath, I watched as she clenched her chest, struggling to suck air into her lungs. Like always, I froze on the spot until her labored breathing subsided into a soft wheeze. Five or ten minutes passed before she was able to continue.

"Remember, Dawnie, I told you 'bout the heavy crane accident that killed my husband? Your mother was just ten years old when she lost her daddy. I had no choice but to take her and her brother, Tom, out of school and move us into that old tenement building down on the lower west side of the Bronx. I got me some work being a building superintendent trading for a free basement apartment."

"It was cold and dark in those rooms 'cause we never got no windows for the sun to shine warmth in. Jesus, Mary, and Joseph, those basement apartments was so damp, but, thanks-be-to-God, we had us a roof over our heads. Your mother's always been a hard worker, Dawnie, collecting the rent money from those grumpy old tenants, treating her like it was our fault that life was so hard and they got stuck living in them ugly old rooms."

Gritting my teeth with mixed hatred toward my mother, I wondered if that was one of the things that made her so mean. Grandmother continued, "Roland admired your mother's grit; he wanted to marry her and promised one day he would bring her home to meet his parents. He knew she'd be all right with his father, but not his prudish mother. 'No,' said Roland, 'an uneducated, feisty, Irish Catholic girl would never pass my mother's inspection; as soon as she opened her mouth they knowed she can't talk good.' They was French Canadian, Presbyterian, and had proper education. Roland talked about this worry with me when your mother was out shopping or collecting rent money. But you know me, I never give advice. Besides, what could I say, Dawnie, he was talking about my daughter. Oh, I knew plenty of those high-falutin' women like his mother in my time. Think they be better than the rest of us just 'cause they speak good. My heart ached for both them children."

Grandma's nondescript, sort of grayish, eye color seemed to turn a different shade right before me as she continued to reminisce, staring into the distance and remembering the past as she continued to tell the story.

"Shame they never had a chance to work it out. His proposal and meeting up with his family was delayed by Uncle Sam. They were both just kids in 1939 when he got called to go overseas. You know, Honey, he said he wrote your mother some five hundred thirty-two letters that never got answered by your mother—'cause she never got 'em, don't you see. He said his guts burned with anger at her silence. Some cruel act of fate, or somethin', the letters never got delivered to your mother. Can you imagine such a thing? It surely is a life mystery."

Grandma stood and lit a candle on the altar, just to the right of Mother Mary's feet. I loved when she lit candles: it made our bedroom seem safe and cozy, even if the room was already filled with so much cigarette smoke my eyes burned. Continuing, she said, "Back home in New York, your mother waited for a whole year, barely able to take a breath, waiting for a word, any word, from her Roland. She tried to track him down through the military, but they were no help at all, them ones. She had to think that he changed his mind about loving her. She even wondered how she could have been so wrong about Roland loving her."

"A year of silence gone by, when one day your mother told me that she knowed two things for sure. She had to move on and that she would never love no other man the way she loved your father."

Grandma looked at me and sort of shook her head as if just realizing that she was sitting there telling me this story. I was afraid that she would stop talking, but she continued, "So, when a kind and handsome Marine, by the name of Ski, kept pestering your mother for her hand in marriage, promising to take care of her and me forever, your mother agreed to his proposal. She did it in a beholden way, 'cause he was so good to her and to me, but she was always guilty knowing that her heart belonged to her Roland."

"Ski and your mother married quickly because he was leaving soon. Right away, your mother got pregnant with your brother, Ronnie, and Ski was shipped out to sea. Finally, your mother was no longer considered an old maid, and we had enough money from Ski's paychecks. Ronnie was born while Ski was to sea."

Squishing out her cigarette in hard little jabs, my grandma seemed agitated as she pushed on with her story. "Three long years passed, and then one day we got word that Ski had died on a battleship somewhere in the Pacific Ocean; your mother heard he died from some mysterious foreign disease. He only got to see his son one time, when on leave, before he died on the ship. Oh, how proud he was of his boy. He was a fine young man, that Ski."

"She didn't grieve much, though, because within a few days of your mother hearing 'bout Ski's death, Roland got home from the war. It was a really hard time for our country, Dawnie; nothin' would ever be the same no more." Grandma sounded sad and far away again. It was as if this long-ago experience had broken her just as much as it had broken my mother. I felt if I reached out to touch her, she would disappear into a chasm of unreachable sorrow. It scared me when she talked as if she were alone in the room.

"Your mother was so happy to be with Roland again, Dawnie, and right away she got pregnant with you." With a weary sadness, my grandmother went on with her story, but I noticed now that her shoulders were bent over as if the weight of the world was pushing on them. I wanted to put my arms around her, to comfort her, but I was fearful that she would stop talking. God help me, I desperately needed to know this story. Grandmother went on, clearly struggling with the heaviness that the remembering caused her. I felt guilty for pushing her, but I had to know the truth. I had been told for my entire fourteen years that my biological father was Ski Laskovitch, even though I never believed that.

A feeling of foreboding began as I started thinking about my true paternity and how I might not be totally bound as brother and sister with Ronnie. Did this mean that my precious big brother was not my *whole* brother, just my half-brother? What did that mean anyway? Does "half-brother" mean less of a brother? I fought to keep down the tears; I did not want to interrupt the story again.

Grandma went on, "Both were broken and scarred real bad from their different experiences. Neither of them understood 'bout the lost letters, but in the end it didn't matter anyway, because Roland had hardened his heart to the love that he once felt for your mother. Who can say if it was the years gone by, or his time in the war, but he was surely a changed man. Said he felt betrayed that she'd married another man and had his child. He thought her to be damaged merchandise. You know, Dawnie, men had some strange ideas in those days. If touched by another man, the woman was considered damaged goods. You have to be a virgin or you are spoiled—so you remember that, Honey. They courted for a while, but when she told him that she was pregnant with his child, you know—he mistrusted her. He said the child could not be his. He offered to help with an abortion, but said there would never be no marriage." Grandma looked at me with such tenderness in her eyes as she asked, "Are you sure that you want me to continue?"

"Yup," I said.

"The day after telling Roland 'bout being pregnant with you, he hightailed it out of New York City. Rumor had it that in six weeks he married a new woman. Know how your mother never gets tired of that song "Who's Sorry Now?" Well, now you know why. What's really awful here, Dawnie, is that your mother has never been the same girl that she was before this hurt. Broken hearts makes people be different in all kinds of strange ways; some people never get put back right once broken apart like that."

Tears trickled down her cheeks as she said, "Honey, that is why I always ask you to pray for your mother and not pay too much attention to her craziness. She's just never been right since losing Roland."

Suddenly, sitting up straight and looking into my eyes, she quickly added, "But in no way would your mother abort her child, a child she made in love. With a heart so broken, we were not sure that it could ever get mended. Your mother quickly made up a plan that would fix that mortal sin weighing on her soul. She wanted to protect you, Dawnie. Taking the bus across the United States and getting settled there in California, where no one knew her sin, fixed everything in her thinking. We always knowed God forgived her sin, but the Church and nosy neighbors were very harsh in those days. 'Specially when you could see people's sins big as life.

"We stayed there in Redlands until you be three months old, then moved to San Diego where your mother would have a better chance to find her a sailor to marry and to adopt you. Dawnie, in those days, the child was considered a bastard and that was really bad. No one had no use for a bastard child. But your mother would have none of that for her baby. She would stop at nothing to save her child from having the bastard name tied to her little neck."

Grandma's face turned ashen as she continued speaking, so softly that I had to lean forward to hear her words, "So after a short stay in Redlands to get you borned, with no money, little food, and scared out of her mind, your mother waved good-bye to me. Holding you in my arms, and your brother Ronnie holding tight to my hand, I was scared to death for her. We was to follow soon after she got settled in a place to live, new job and all. The bravest thing she ever did, Dawnie. I was sick with worry about your mother; I can tell you that, child."

We both put out our cigarettes and sat in silence, watching the Jesus, Mary, and Joseph statues as if they could somehow console us.

As we were sitting there, a pebble smacked up against the window. I said, "Oh, no, Grandma, I'm late." We both started giggling as she helped me sneak out of the bedroom window, where Ross was waiting.

Ross and I needed to meet as we were practicing our jitterbug steps for the upcoming dance on Saturday night. We were good dancers.

As Grandma closed the window, I promised to be back in an hour.

The Early Sixties

NINETEEN YEARS MY senior, Marilyn Monroe's images did not *consciously* influence my life, yet for as long as I can remember her voluptuous silhouette coexisted with my formative years. Images of her sexual receptivity proliferated in television and magazines. When I was seventeen, her shadow traversed my budding sexuality and haunted my first sexual experiences with my young husband. I married her stepson, Joey, within six months of her death.

All around me, freedom abounded during the early sixties. Girls (not me) were wearing bikinis for the first time. Sexual freedom became more common and open. Opinions about Vietnam were heated. Betty Friedan was a leading figure in this *second wave* of the U.S. women's movement (the first wave of feminism being women's right to vote). In her 1963 book *The Feminine Mystique*, Friedan talks about the prevailing unhappiness of a large portion of women during the fifties and sixties. Men seem to believe at that time that women should be fulfilled solely by the role of homemaker. If women were not happy, they were considered neurotic or mentally unstable.

In reaction to these prevailing expectations of women, particularly to contribute physically and financially during WWII then demurely retreat back to the kitchen and housewifery, a culture backlash occurred in the sixties. Some refer to this period as the time of sex, drugs, and rock and roll. I thought women should have the right to aspire to whatever they wanted to do or be in life, so the early sixties were a confusing time for me.

Prior to my first marriage, I was busy protecting my virginity, and obsessed with the endeavor to learn to behave the way that I thought a lady was suppose to act—not because of some great virtue, but in order to overcome what people thought of me. Also, I thought that chastity would matter to my future husband.

Preserving a woman's virginity may sound trite by today's moral standards; however, in many parts of the world, even today, women are murdered for losing their virginity, even if by rape.

My father refused to marry my mother. He considered her used merchandise because she had married another. A boy in high school said that his mother forbade his seeing me. I was not made of the right stuff, was assumed to be loose. From these prevailing attitudes, I concluded a woman's value was based solely upon her being unspoiled.

Chaste. Pure. Is it any wonder that I wanted to hide my body, my sexuality, my sensuality?

In between my first and second marriage (both at age nineteen), I was bewildered by all that was happening around me culturally: President Kennedy's assassination, ambiguous messages embedded in music like Bob Dylan's "Blowing in the Wind," hippies, and the Vietnam War. During my stewardess days, I was deeply affected by the vacant stare I witnessed in the eyes of the young men returning from war. They reminded me of my dad Howard's empty stares and unreachable heart. Nightmares of brooding, dark eyes haunted me. I was also totally mystified by the notion of sexual freedom without guilt. My second husband demanded modesty. My first husband resented my reserve. How to be in a world of men? In a world dominated by men? Oh, how was I to be a woman?

Surprisingly, Marilyn loved, even flaunted, her nudity openly. There are many reports of her saying that she did not receive much pleasure from the sexual act itself. "Sex was less a reward to herself than a price she paid gladly," says Gloria Steinem.

Experts in child development concur that when girls are exposed to sexuality too young, they may become sexually compulsive. The sense of power their sexuality affords them can become addictive when they're seeking attention from men. Other girls may turn their reaction *inward* by going to the opposite extreme, thinking and behaving in ultra-modest ways. And so it was with Norma Jeane's response in contrast to mine.

Marilyn repeatedly stated that she just wanted to be noticed, as reflected in this quote: "I daydreamed chiefly about beauty. I dreamed of myself becoming so beautiful that people would turn to look at me when I passed." By most people's standards, she attained that goal with outstanding success.

It has been said that we grow in the eyes of an *other*, that we in fact need others to call us into being. I believe that the camera was that "other" for Marilyn. It may have been the only "eye" that ever really saw her. She never had the mirroring of safe eyes as a child or as an adult—only that ever-present camera lens, the eye that lit up her life.

***

At age nineteen—deeply confused, but at the same time in the throes of budding self-esteem—I thought my life was under my control. But following in shades of Marilyn, I became promiscuous, and a drunk, and I attempted suicide. How far I would fall from my own ideals.

In retrospect, I can understand Joey's attraction to me. I hold within my being many of the psychological imprints and traits of Marilyn, the stepmother he idolized. Like her, I was mired in the insecurities of deep wounds, fostered and sustained in the constant atmosphere of illegitimacy, illiteracy, family instability, and societal judgments. And, like Marilyn, I was street-smart but ignorant in worldly matters such as formal education, social class, customs, dress, and manners.

> "I knew how third rate I was. I could actually feel my lack of talent, as if it were cheap clothes I was wearing inside."
>
> —Marilyn

Simultaneously vulnerable and tough, I grew quite capable of taking care of my basic survival needs. Like Marilyn, I attracted men who wanted to take care of me. We both seemed to emit mixed signals that would convey "Come here and take care of me," and "Go away, I don't need you."

Marilyn and I had the profound instability of emotions, embedded deeply within us, that tend to create a pervasive vulnerability among girls who are abused in early childhood. This vulnerability is often palatable to those around us, no matter the calloused exterior we present. I think Joey unconsciously chose me based on this sense of fragility, coupled with his desire to recreate the warmth that he felt in Marilyn's presence. He told me that she was one of the few adults who really saw him or paid any personal attention to him. She became his family when Joey lived with his father and Monroe after the two married. She ended up being connected to her stepson for the rest of her life. Joey spoke with Marilyn the night she died. He absolutely adored her.

Growing Up in Marilyn's Shadow

WITH NINETEEN YEARS separating us, I was only a toddler, just learning to *say* my name, when Norma Jeane was getting used to signing autographs with the new name Twentieth Century Fox Studios had made up for her: MARILYN MONROE. Before I suffered the embarrassment of needing my first training bra, Marilyn was making it obvious that the more a girl had "up top" and was willing to show it off, the more she would be remembered and sought after.

I grew up in an era when morale-boosting "pinup girl" pictures, like the nude that had rocketed Norma Jeane out of obscurity, had found a showplace in the girly magazines that were as ordinary as ashtrays on living room coffee tables. Back then, no one thought of smoking as dangerous to your health, and no one thought of magazines with names like *Titter*, *Peek*, *See*, and *Cheesecake* as pornography. I remember seeing such magazines displayed right alongside *Life* and the *Saturday Evening Post* on magazine stands. Society just dismissed them with the age-old permissive adage that "boys will be boys."

During the late forties and all through the fifties, Marilyn, clothed in the most revealing bathing suits of the time and striking the most provocative poses she could get away with, graced the covers of many of these magazines. And then, in 1953, when the first issue of *Playboy* made its daring debut, its first completely nude centerfold was of Marilyn, in all her glory, stretched across a field of red velvet.

Her blatant sexuality caused me to burn with a shame that I was too young to understand. Images of her in one degree of undress or another flooded the media for the first seventeen years of my life, and I remember feeling disgusted by her. It seemed to me that she was everything I never wanted to be. She was *not* "ladylike" the way 1950s Home Economics classes and my Catholic upbringing insisted a woman should be. She flaunted her sexuality outrageously, and seemed delighted that she was lusted after. I hated the "dumb blond sexpot" stereotype that she seemed to enjoy. After all, I was a blonde, and I was dumb, at least according to my school IQ tests. But I certainly didn't have her beauty or sex appeal which kept people's attention, if not their respect. She was everything I had come to understand a woman should never be. I made it a goal to be as disdainful of her as I could, and to deliberately avert my eyes from her.

I was fifteen when I went to see Marilyn in the movie *Let's Make Love*—one of her most blatantly sexual films. I went because I wanted to fit in with some of my friends from school. What I really wanted to do more than anything was have an excuse to sit next to one particular boy. Too naïve to realize that no male in that theater was going to be thinking of me while Marilyn was on the screen, I had such a crush on him that I was willing to endure Marilyn's celluloid persona if it meant that I could be close to him for a whole hour and a half. Her goal was to be desired by every male who ever laid eyes on her. Who could think of anything else during the movie when she slid down a pole wearing nothing but a tight blue sweater and no pants? My face burned so hot I thought it must be glowing in the dark—but even if it had been, no one would have noticed.

***

Staring down at my clenched fists in my lap, I tried to force Marilyn's sensuality out of my mind and my body; but it didn't work, thanks to the stupid song she sang in a voice dripping with sexual innuendo, "My heart belongs to Da-Da-Da-Daddy." The thought of any of the several "daddies" I have had in my life doing anything sexual to me nearly made my stomach turn.

In another scene, her skintight dress left nothing to the imagination—except maybe how her breasts could possibly be as pointy as they appeared. And then her voice, so sugary and sappy, and her body language, every inch of which made you think she wanted to devour every man she saw. I could sense the young man sitting next to me getting excited, as if pheromones were spilling out every time he exhaled. I was beyond mortified! I detested how she used her sexuality to make being a woman the equivalent of being a slut, someone who men both lusted after and despised. As my friends and I walked out of the theater after the movie and I listened to them—especially the boys—talk about her in such cheap, vulgar language, I felt like the sidewalk was tilted under my feet. Folding my arms tightly across my chest, I walked a step behind the others, trying to repress my disgust.

***

And then suddenly, on August 4, 1962, Marilyn Monroe was dead, accidentally overdosing on alcohol and drugs. When I heard this, I thought, *Well, there you go, Norma Jeane. That's exactly what a girl gets when she wants too much.* That was my seventeen-year-old interpretation of what was screwed up about Marilyn—she had wanted too much, given away too much, and settled for too little. Even though I had come from such similar circumstances, I would never allow myself to act or be like Marilyn. I turned my rigid idealism into the caption for my senior picture: "Never want too much out of life, but never accept too little."

***

What I didn't realize was that Marilyn's blatant immodesty repulsed me because of something else that we shared. Before either of us were nine, we had been traumatized by adult men who made us objects of their thoughtless lust.

While she seemed to be shameless about exposing her body in public—even to the point of nudity—I became so terrified to be seen in the nude that by the time I was in high school, I couldn't bring myself to undress and shower in front of other girls in my Physical Education classes.

In the 1950s, dressing out and participating in a P.E. class was mandatory every semester throughout high school, as was stripping and showering before you could go on to your next class. I use the word showering loosely: for most girls, the act amounted to wrapping one of the small white towels around their hair and running through the communal shower area between blasting shower heads. In order to keep track of who showered, the gym staff gave every girl a plastic ring along with her towel each day. If your ring wasn't hanging on the wooden board at the far end of the shower area, on the peg corresponding to your locker number, you were given an "F" for the day, even if you had dressed out and participated in the day's activities.

***

"Hey, Tammy," I whisper to the stark-naked girl next to me in the steamy locker room, wearing only a towel draped around her neck. She is just about to close her locker and head for the running showers. There really isn't any reason for me to lower my voice, since the air is filled with several dozen girls' voices, all talking and laughing loud enough to be heard above the hiss of the dozen showerheads. But I don't want our gym teachers to hear me offer Tammy cigarettes as a bribe for what I desperately need her to do for me.

She acts like she hasn't heard me. I start to panic. Maybe she's going to ignore me. After all, we're not really friend-friends. More like locker-room acquaintances. In fact, she's one of the "in-crowd," while I'm the furthest thing from it. "Tammy," I begin again, still keeping my voice low, trying to communicate that I am about to say something that needs to be treated with more than a little stealth, "I need a *huge* favor and I have some cigarettes I could give you."

Tammy pauses in her locker-stuffing effort, glances over her shoulder at me, and waits for me to finish my sentence. Now I have her attention, and for good reason: cigarettes are the gold standard of contraband among most girls in the school, which puts me in a sweet position. Back at home, my grandma has been sharing her smokes with me since I was twelve the way most grandmas would share candy. Even when I put a handful in my purse to take to school, she never says a word.

I hold out the plastic ring. Tammy knows what I want her to do; this isn't the first time I have asked. Still, she has to mull over her decision. If she gets caught it could mean some serious consequences for both of us. And the chances of her getting caught could be pretty high if one or the other of our gym teachers is sitting in the doorway of the shower room, supervising us while we shower. I don't care what they call it, I can't stomach getting naked and running the gauntlet. More than once, on days when the teachers were paying too-close attention and I couldn't get anyone to put my ring on its peg, I've become so upset I had to retreat to the toilet stalls and vomit.

Tammy glances at me and leans around the end of the locker row, looking both ways to see if she can tell where our gym teachers are. Apparently, she thinks she has seen both of them, because she turns back to me and holds out her hand to take my ring. We both know we are risking suspension if we are caught—but Tammy wants the cigarettes almost as bad as I want to avoid getting naked. Taking my ring from me, Tammy puts it with her own ring and turns toward the showers. I watch as she falls in with some other girls going in at the same time and starts acting as if she's been part of their chatter and laughter all along. Clever.

For a minute I sit still and listen. A minute is usually about all the time it takes for a girl to get through the shower and to the board and hang up her ring. Suddenly I hear our assistant gym teacher, Miss James, yelling—almost screeching—Tammy's name.

"Tammy! Tammy Davis! What are you doing?"

There's no more chatter. No laughing. Even the sound of the showers seems to have faded almost to nothing. Still, I have no trouble hearing Tammy's trembling voice, "N . . . n . . . nothing, Miss James."

"Don't you lie to me, Tammy Davis. I saw you put Veronica's ring on its peg."

When I hear Miss James use my given name, I know I'm dead. Usually everyone calls me by my nickname, Ronnie. Damn! How'd she know it was *my* peg? As if all the teachers didn't have *my* number memorized by this point in the semester.

My shoulders sink as I hear Tammy crying and begging, "Please don't suspend me, Miss James. My dad will kill me. I promise not to do it ever again."

Miss James' tone of voice is almost back to normal as she continues, but I can still hear her as if she were standing right beside me. "Well I hope you and Grace (Miss James' favorite sarcastic nickname for me) are going to learn a lesson from this, because I am suspending both of you."

I clutch my towel to my chest, despite being fully clothed. The girls up and down my locker aisle are all looking at me, and I feel as good as naked. They're the lucky ones, the normal ones. The ones that can blow off getting naked. And now they're the ones who can finish dressing and rush out to spread the story to everyone who will listen—which, of course, will be everyone. By lunchtime, I'll be the butt of a hundred jokes and the object of everyone's stares. Without warning, my breakfast rises up into my throat, and I run for the toilet stalls.

***

Tammy may have had to face her dad with the news that she had been suspended for the rest of the week, but that was nothing compared to what I was certain would happen to me if I got suspended too many times and failed P.E.: the looming threat of having to drop out of high school. Tammy might get a whippin' for what she did, but I felt like my hope to ever have a life would be destroyed if I didn't get through high school. I was already hoping for a miracle just to graduate. Besides, what kind of idiot fails P.E.? That's how all my peers felt about it, and it was definitely how I felt about it. Failing P.E. would confirm to me what a negative, downright evil voice from somewhere inside me seemed to hiss at me every day: that I was nothing but a "dumpster-diving, trailer-trash kid—a klutz, a fool, a joke, a lazy-ass moron."

Never able to control my terror of being naked in front of other people, there were days when I couldn't face going to school at all because of P.E., which never concerned my mother. After all, she hadn't finished high school. She was a child of the 1920s, and a girl child—just like Norma Jeane. She remembered all too well growing up in the Depression and then suffering the death-blow that World War II had been to her hopes and dreams. School just didn't seem that important.

There was one excuse I could give my mother for needing a note to excuse me from P.E. When my period started, I would tell her in terms she understood: "I got sick, Mom." I used the expression, even though I thought it was stupid and old-fashioned. I preferred "I got my period." My mother was rendered bed-ridden with her periods, so she sympathized with me. It was true that some months I *would* suffer from extreme and severe menstrual cramps and heavy flow. I kept my terror of nudity from my mother and my grandmother, which left me all alone with my horror and with the childhood memories that fueled it. There was no way I could ever tell my mother about the grown men who had "played" with me in the years since I was seven, or how their groping, fondling attention to my nakedness had left me obsessed with avoiding exposing myself to others. I knew that not getting a high school diploma would affect my whole life, but vomiting from terror and maybe even dying from the shame of my nudity was too much for me to face.

With the mixture of desperation and gratitude of a drowning soul I leapt at the school district's summer school P.E. program. You didn't have to take a public shower in summer school. You could just go home, sweat and all.

Spiderwebs

AT SIXTEEN I felt sorry for my mother and grandmother's bleak lives, but I desperately wanted to leave the house. I felt mired in a spiderweb of yuck. This was made worse by their close friendship with the most disgusting person I had ever met. My stomach turned every time I saw her, which was often.

June White had crusty, light brown hair that spilled its dandruff everywhere. Her face and arms were covered in open sores and she stunk. She always smelled like twenty-year-old sheets might if they were stuffed into an old pillowcase, yellowed by age, and forgotten amidst spiderwebs in a filthy garage. June had regressed into a physical depository of ills since we had met her eight years before.

When I was six or seven, I sometimes visited my friend, Sara. We would sit on the floor, watching cartoons on the small television in her unkempt living room. There was no available vacant space to be found in the living room, dining room, or kitchen, since magazines, dirty clothes, cigarette butts, and encrusted dishes cluttered every bit of space. June, Sara's mother, would hum mindlessly as her head was bent over her sewing machine, absorbed with her dearly loved swatches of colorful material. She caressed them and talked to them as if they were real family members. She cherished her fabric the way I always imagined a mother was meant to love her children.

One day the door to the bedroom was left ajar, and I could see Jane, the oldest daughter, her body being kneaded the way I'd seen bread prepared on television. Low grunts erupted from the mouth of Jane's father, who was atop her. At that age, I didn't exactly understand what was happening, but everything inside my body recoiled at this mysterious, frightening scene. I was certain that something was wrong, but could not for the life of me figure it out.

Watching with a feeling of foreboding, I looked from the television, to the mother, to the little sister, to the bedroom, and back, again and again. I tried to reconcile what I was witnessing with the feelings that I was experiencing, but I never succeeded. I left that house feeling as if I were going to gag on the little pieces of June White's fabric.

I don't recall when, or how, I finally told my grandmother what I had witnessed, but I did eventually tell her. Since no one in my family ever mentioned this situation again to explain what had happened, it left me feeling even more confused, just as the time would come when no one spoke to me about the incident with dear old Uncle Bill.

Toward the end of my fourteenth year, my mother persuaded my grandmother to take a weekend trip with the family. We would drive to Los Angeles from San Diego and visit their oldest friends from New York. Aunt Hazel had known my grandmother when my mother was just a girl. Her son Bill and my mother grew up together. Mother and grandmother were very excited about the trip, and I was excited to have them leave the house for a change.

After dinner, visiting, and television shows I was escorted to a comfortable cot in the laundry room. With a full tummy, I immediately fell fast asleep.

I awoke to suffocating alcohol breaths and wet lips covering my mouth. This man, this distant uncle they called Bill, was now calling me filthy names as his large hands tried to grope me.

"Get out of here or I will scream!"

"What the matter with you, girly? You think that a slut like you is too good for me? Well let me tell you sumpin, you little bastard."

Jumping off the cot and backing up against the wall, my heart was pounding out of my chest while I fought his hands off me. I said, "I mean it, I swear to God I will start screaming if you don't get away from me."

He backed away and left. I stood against the wall wondering for the millionth time how everyone seemed to know about that bastard thing. Then the sound of a gun: Uncle Bill had committed suicide.

I watched as men in white wheeled his blood-soaked body out the door. I told my mother and grandmother what had happened, but was met with silence. In spite of their silence, I somehow knew from a deep place within that I had not caused his suicide. What remained confusing was that the families continued reminiscing about, "Dear old Uncle Bill" as if the incident had never happened. It seemed to me at the time that the importance of his good memory was clearly more important than the truth of what actually took place just before the gunshot.

Barely fifteen, I assumed a budding new sense of pride in myself by saying no to Uncle Bill, even though the unwelcome echo of the gunshot diminished that feeling. It seemed like a haunting refrain that taunted me for years to come. How I wished just one adult would have told me it wasn't my fault.

***

So the memory of June's husband molesting her daughter and the nightmare of Uncle Bill were with me as I watched June oozing herself into our living room. I always felt as if her dull, brown, preying eyes were secretly watching me. Like the victim of a black widow spider, I was sure if she looked at me she could ensnare me in a web of poison. It didn't help that the inevitable conversation made my stomach feel as though it were absorbing sticky venom from the air.

June, in her high-pitched, whining voice, would describe her latest doctor's visit with some warm-up, get-ready-for-it, I-can-be-even-more-detailed prefaces: "Well, the doctor said that I just had to get more rest to protect my bad heart."

So then my mother, excited about contributing *her* misery, would reply with glee, "Last week, the doctor told me that I had diabetes. So now I have to take these certain medications, along with eating better." (During this time, our main food was TV dinners or some drop-off food from the Salvation Army.) "Of course, I also need to rest more."

On cue, I'd hear my grandmother having an asthma attack. Knowing that she held a cigarette in one hand, she would take her other hand and remove her inhaler from her ever-present, five-pocket apron. She would place the container in her mouth, shut her eyes, and inhale deeply. The routine never varied. Next, Grandma, pushing on through her laborious breathing, voice weak with suffering, would reply to Mother's new health advisory, "But you know that I will take care of you, Veronica."

At this point, I stuffed a pillow over my head so I wouldn't hear any more of the hypochondriacal exchange. I was fuming, angry that my sickly grandmother waited hand and foot on my mother, who rarely left the living room couch. For years I watched her shuffle from the kitchen to the couch, meeting my mother's every demand. I adored my grandmother, and I railed against my mother's demands for service.

***

From age fifteen through seventeen, the years passed uneventfully. By the time I was sixteen, my mother, grandmother, younger brother, and I were living in a decent neighborhood. I was working and going to school—well, sometimes.

I was earning my own money through various jobs such as housekeeping for neighbors, babysitting, and ironing clothes. Thanks to a few severely decayed teeth that I had to have extracted, I was forced into my first visit to a dentist. He said to me, "Young lady, at the rate of your tooth decay, by the time you are twenty-one you won't have a tooth left in your mouth." After explaining that we were on welfare and I had no way of paying to have my teeth fixed, the dentist offered to fix the rest of my decaying teeth in exchange for babysitting his young children on an ongoing basis. I leaped at the opportunity and was proud of my resourcefulness as my pretty new smile emerged, which added greatly to my budding self-confidence.

As my confidence and self-sufficiency grew, I was beginning to have more dates than I had time for. I controlled the kissing part of the date so that most of my suitors didn't try anything else, except for one time when a boy tried to force himself on me. When he tried to force me I bit his cheek so hard I could taste the blood. The pain forced him to loosen his grip and I escaped into the night, running through the canyon until I found help.

I may not have fit in with the *in crowd*, but it was a big school, and I had lots of friends. I went to *six* senior proms, starting when I was a freshman. Girlfriends loaned me beautiful dresses, and I worked enough odd jobs to afford to have my long hair put up into a pretty bouffant for the dances. My self-confidence grew to a point that I even taught a group of developmentally challenged girls at school how to fix their hair, and I couldn't have cared less if other kids made fun of me.

So I was taken aback during my junior year to discover that many folks still recalled my old house with no paint.

I think back sometimes to a conversation that I had with a boy at school. He was seventeen, I was sixteen. His name was Finn Z. He drove a cherry red roadster, which was the envy of every boy in school. Each day, at lunchtime, his eyes, the color of the sky, met mine across the cafeteria. Finally, one day in the parking lot, he offered to drive me home after school.

He said, "I would love to take you out but my mother won't allow it. I'll be in big trouble today if she hears that I even had you in my car."

"Why?" My jaw slackened.

He said, "Because of your reputation."

Mortified, I said, "But I haven't done anything, Finn."

"But people assume that you have because of your past."

"I'm still a virgin." Like a frantic child trying to show my worth, I said, "I could prove it by going to the doctor."

He smiled kindly as he slowly shook his head, "People remember where you grew up, and your family. . ." and his voice slowly trailed off into silence. I could tell how uncomfortable he was saying these things; though shame-filled, I didn't feel I was being judged by this young man. I thanked him for the ride, and we said our good-byes with sadness. For the rest of the school year we continued our tender glances across the cafeteria, but we never spoke again.

Embarrassed by Finn's words, I wrote this poem:

> She was forbidden to date the elite who proclaimed dirt
> and chipped paint was embedded into her core.
>
> While she endeavored to hold her head high, she knew her place,
> one step back, the appropriate place among those filled with
> inherited grace. Her virginity still in place
>
> afforded defiance against her invisible disgrace. THIS was her
> visible badge of honor. She valiantly fought anyone who
> dared tarnish it. She consecrated herself
>
> to the one who would come someday—her Prince, her savior.
> In the piercing of the veil, redemption would prevail. She readied
>
> for HIM, which made it possible for her to endure THEM.
>
> He would know of her innocence and grant her absolution
> for the sins she never committed.

How desperately I wanted to be redeemed. But I believed that redemption came from the outside. I needed someone, anyone, to stamp me whole, like an accused prisoner found innocent.

Desperate to Launch

MY MOTHER REMAINED under her blanket of depression, rarely leaving the living room couch. Her world revolved around television, food, pills, and juggling bills. She vigilantly divided our scarce money into little white envelopes.

Since my mother and grandmother had become recluses, I became their connection with the outside world. Mother had given up on men and any hope of ever getting a job. Memories of my father became her lover. Like a sunny day, I became an occasional diversion. Grandmother seemed content with her Bible, cigarettes, and television sports.

God, the New York Yankees, and wrestling matches with Gorgeous George on the small black-and-white TV were everything my grandmother ever needed. There she'd be, elbows extended out over her large, oblong breasts as she rested them on her little, bony knees, her rosary beads hanging from her left hand, cigarette hanging from her lips, right hand balled up into a fist, shaking it at the TV screen screaming "Kill him, kill him!" as Gorgeous George would lift his opponent over his head and slam him onto the mat. Sometimes she got so excited that her false teeth fell out of her mouth right onto the floor, sending me and my brother into fits of laughter.

It was such an incongruent sight to behold, as she was otherwise the meekest woman that I had ever known, never raising her voice. When the wrestling match was over, she shuffled into the tiny kitchen, shut the door, and read her Bible, which concluded her afternoon ritual. Her behavior and the sequence of her actions never once seemed unusual to her, nor did she understand our uproarious laughter during these most prized sporting events.

I spent enormous amounts of energy thinking of ways to entertain them. Anything to make them smile. I felt sad that their lives seemed so profoundly bleak. Making up stories for entertainment, I embellished on little things that happened throughout my day. Constantly searching for ways to ease my mother's unhappiness and abate her angry outbursts consumed much of my energy. Like a regurgitating parrot, I told her what she wanted to hear, that she was a wonderful mother and I was so very grateful to be her daughter, blah, blah, blah.

I continued my placating behaviors for years after moving away from home. Playacting and appeasing became a second nature to me. After my mother died, I ran across some of the letters that I had sent her. I felt sick when I read what I had written: words drenched in phony "happy talk" and dripping with flattery. In every letter, I gave her a report of my current weight, apologetic if I weighed one pound over the amount with which *she* felt comfortable. During my teenage years, perhaps because her own weight ballooned toward the two hundred-pound mark as she sank deeper into her plastic-covered couch, she became obsessed with my weight. For some obscure reason, my mother equated my weight with my value as a person, and I tried to accommodate her.

During my entire childhood, my brother Ronnie was the family hero. He alone held our mother's attention and delight. Because I also adored him, I never questioned his special place. He was my hero as well.

After Ronnie left for the Marines, I suddenly replaced him as the unlikely family hero. Like the bull's-eye on a target, Mother now focused fully on me. Her unexpected attention was both thrilling and disconcerting: thrilling because I had her undivided attention, and disturbing because she now honed in on my physical appearance. She began lightening my hair. She thought that blondes fared better in the world of men. We chatted like girlfriends as she applied the bleach while I blew smoke rings from Grandma's Kool cigarettes. Suddenly, I felt special. Heady stuff for a thirteen-year-old. Still, a part of me knew that I couldn't trust this camaraderie. One night, when I was fifteen, I came home from a date filled with delight because "Johnny" had said that I was pretty. I told my mother what he had said.

Mother quipped, "Dawn, you are not pretty. You are interesting-looking, but you are certainly not pretty." Her words hurt my feelings, but she was my mother, after all, so she must know the truth. Years later, a therapist asked me what I saw when I looked in a mirror. I replied, "A cheap-looking blonde with hard eyes."

I joined my mother in her all-out effort to make me pretty, even if it seemed she owned me like one owns chattel. I felt like she was grooming her property for some future payoff on her investment. I hated her. I loved her. I needed her. I needed her desperately. I hated her.

I felt smothered in her expectations, demands, melancholy and unspoken depression. I desperately wanted to escape.

Except for those times when I could entertain her with embellished stories or she was engaged in dissecting my appearance, she was lost in the plastic beige couch and her memories. Her obsession with the loss of my biological father was stunning: she glowed every time she heard the popular song "Who's Sorry Now?"

While she obsessed about her one and only love, I obsessed about the day, the hour, and the method of my escape from her tentacles.

***

When that day arrived, I told my mother I wanted to move out. She became unhinged.

"Mom, I will be getting an apartment with a girlfriend when I graduate."

"What did you just say, Dawn?" I noticed that her face had suddenly turned dark.

"I said that I am moving out, Mom."

Her voice became shrill, sounding only partially human. She screamed, "Why you ungrateful little brat, I have given up my entire life for you. I have sacrificed everything to give you a name and a home. How dare you talk to me this way?"

Recoiling from the blast, I pleaded, "Mom, *Mom*, I do appreciate everything that you have done for me, but I just want to begin my own life when I turn eighteen."

She continued screaming: "Your life! *Your* life! You don't have a life. You will stay here and contribute to this family. We need the money, do you understand me? Where do you get off being so selfish?"

As compensation for her sacrifices, I would be expected to give her my paycheck—"under the table," of course. That way we wouldn't lose any of our welfare benefits. "Mom, *pleeease*, I just want to start my own life."

Shrieking, my mother yelled, "Now you listen to me, young lady, I don't want to hear another word out of your dirty mouth. As of today, you're restricted to this house until you start thinking straight. You may go to work and school, but nothing else. Do you understand?"

I had not been on restriction since junior high school. I came and went at whatever hours I wanted. Although I had always called my mother with the phone numbers of where I would be, she never suggested a curfew. So now she was placing me on restriction because I wanted to start my own life? I was furious with what seemed a grave injustice.

Usually obedient, I slammed out of the house.

I didn't know it when I ran out the door, but my whole life would change that afternoon when I met Joey, my prince.

The Prince Arrives

MY FIVE-MILE WALK to the bowling alley was filled with angry thoughts of my mother and worried thoughts for my grandmother, who had been sucking on her inhaler as I left. If and when I left home for good I would miss her so. Funny how I can remember exactly what I was wearing that day: aqua blue stretch pants with stirrups around the feet and a white, hooded sweater. My hair was pulled up in a twist. Deep in thought, I stared blankly at the empty bowling lanes amidst the mid-morning cleaning. I decided that no matter what happened, I was not going home again until my mother would at least hear me out. Pondering my current predicament in terms of food, shelter, and transportation, I was grateful that it was a Friday: I didn't have to return to my afternoon babysitting job until Monday.

My troubled thoughts were interrupted as two young men sat down, one on either side of me. For a moment I was startled, until I realized one of them was my old high school friend, Tommy. Well over six feet tall, he was one of our best football players.

Tommy and I talked a few minutes about some plans of his that did not turn out as expected. Formalities out of the way, I turned to the other young man and said, "Hi, what's your name?"

"Joe."

"So, Joe, do you know my friend, Tommy?" "No," said Joe with a straight face.

Like an unthinking little fool, I introduced them to each other. They played along with my sincere ignorance until I finally caught on that Joe was lightly punching Tommy in the arm—the way we girls do with boys when they say something that bugs us.

Tommy finally introduced me to his friend, Joey, and mentioned that Joey was living with him and his family.

I asked Joe, "Where are you from?"

"I'm from many places; I went to school back east and in Los Angeles, but I'm currently staying with my friend, Tommy. I am looking for a job and my own place to live." Hanging his head slightly, he said, "So I'm kind of bumming around right now."

"Wow, it sounds like a bad day for all of us. I just had a huge fight with my mother and left home. I'm not going back, either. My mom wants me to help support her. I know that I should, but I just want to live my own life when I graduate in June."

Tommy said, "Ronnie, that's only about three months away. Couldn't you wait until then to leave?"

Feeling overwhelming exhaustion now, I took a deep breath to delay having to respond while I tried to put my thoughts into words. "I don't know, Tommy, my mom said that because of my attitude, I'd be on restriction until I turned eighteen. She's never told me what to do before, and I have never been on restriction. I've dated anyone I wanted to date, set the hour to come home, went where I wanted with who I wanted—and now she's going to dictate to me what to do? I don't know if I can take that. It would be torture for me to be stuck in that house all the time."

I began to notice how handsome this young man named Joe was. Dressed in nice slacks and a casual blue shirt with the sleeves ever-so-carefully rolled up, I could tell that his clothes did not come from our local JC Penney, nor did his loafers. He seemed so sophisticated. Then I looked into his eyes. He met my eyes, and he held them all the while he was talking to me. I had not experienced this feeling of being so seen with any of the other boys that I had dated. I could tell by the way he ate his hot dog, and even the way he unwrapped his straw, that he had good manners. I didn't exactly know what the importance of that was; I just knew that he was different in some kind of a good way. He was mysteriously strong and confident, but not in an arrogant or assuming way.

Particularly struck by the manner in which he spoke, which seemed so *worldly* (although I didn't understand the meaning of some of his words, or what *worldly* might be exactly.) Over the next few hours, he mesmerized me as he engaged me in interesting conversations. Having never been around anyone like him before, I was dazzled by his classiness and intelligence.

When he walked to the counter to buy us hot dogs and Cokes, I thought that he walked with the grace of a panther. As we talked, I found out he was a bodybuilder, an ex-Marine, and had attended Yale.

But it was the way in which he strung words together that delighted me. I was close to illiterate, and had already been diagnosed as borderline retarded, but nevertheless I recognized something beautiful that I had either never heard or simply never noticed before. Words, words, words strung together like effortless poetry. I listened with fascinated attention to every word. In my mind's eye, I imagined a clothesline where, ever-so-carefully, I hung each word slowly, one after the other, to savor later. He said that he liked the "ambiance of the bowling alley."

I envisioned the word "ambiance," and while I couldn't actually spell it, I could remember how the resonance of it echoed in my mind.

He seemed to know everything about everything. I thought him to be brilliant and funny and he made me laugh. I think I fell in love with him before we left the bowling alley four hours later.

The three of us drove around for a few hours, talking, listening to the radio, and imagining the future as only teenagers can do. Then we went to a drive-in restaurant where pretty girls with short skirts and roller skates hung the food tray on the side of the door. Tommy wanted to go to a party that was happening nearby, so Joe and I went with him, but we mostly stayed outside walking and talking. By now, I was calling him "Joey." I couldn't recall his last name.

Later that night, we were standing outside of the car when he kissed me the first time. His kisses were as tender as I imagined babies' eyelashes would be if they were brushing against my lips. I felt I would melt right into the ground each time that he reached for me and put his arms around me. He treated me very tenderly, as if I would break. His tenderness added to my feeling of a relaxed surrender. He, unlike other boys that I sometimes had to fight off, never crossed the line. I never had to block his hands or resist him in any way. He made me feel like a lady, as if he respected me. By this time, after some twelve hours together, he knew that I was a virgin.

Around midnight, Tommy returned to the car and the two of them drove me to the friend's house where I would be staying now that I had "run away." I said good-bye, and began to miss Joey right away. Over the next week, we spent hours upon hours on the phone. If he mentioned his last name during this time it meant nothing to me even though my grandmother had idolized the great ballplayer Joe DiMaggio. He later told me that my initial lack of response to his famous name, and the fact that I had to ask him to repeat it several times during the week, delighted and amused him.

In Love with a Fantasy

INCREDIBLY, I WAS unaware of the fame surrounding my new boyfriend's father, the famous baseball player Joe DiMaggio. A 1969 poll conducted to coincide with the centennial of professional baseball voted him the sport's greatest living player. Songs by famous artists were written about him. One example was a song called "Joltin' Joe DiMaggio," which was written by Alan Courtney and Ben Homer in 1941, and performed by the Les Brown Orchestra. The song was reportedly inspired by his fifty-six-game hitting streak, which led to him being given the nickname "Joltin' Joe DiMaggio." His name was also used in the song "Mrs. Robinson," which was used in the movie *The Graduate*.

Nor did I know of Joey's relationship with his legendary step-mother, Marilyn Monroe, until I returned home after five days "on the lam," so to speak.

I had called my mother from the bowling alley that fateful afternoon and told her I was not coming home, but not to worry: I was safe and would be staying with friends. I knew a lot of kids from school, and it was easy to find various friends to spend the remainder of the week with. Mother was angry, but evidently not worried, because she didn't call the police the entire time I was away. That week, Joey and I became sweethearts. During those first twelve hours that Joey and I spent together, we shared many of our deepest thoughts and feelings with the ease of lifelong friends.

He asked me questions like, "What was it like for you growing up wondering about your father?"

"Well, it's been hard. I think about him all the time. You know, it's like a piece of me is missing and I can't be all of me until I find that missing piece."

"I can understand, because I know who my father is, yet we've never been close and I, too, feel as if there's a piece of me missing."

"How do you mean?"

He breathed in, pursed his lips and blew out his breath, then wistfully said, "Well, if I could know him a little better, then perhaps I'd understand myself a little better."

I remember thinking, *p-e-r-h-a-p-s*, stringing each letter on the imaginary clothesline in my mind. I liked that word, but wondered what it meant exactly in his situation and why did he say that just at that moment?

I asked, "What about your mom? Are you close to her?" "No! We haven't spoken in over a year."

I nuzzled him with my head. "Oh, Joey, that's so sad. Why?"

"I don't know, Dawn. I guess we're both just too occupied with the intricacies in our own lives."

Again, I carefully hung a word, *i-n-t-r-i-c-a-c-i-e-s*, on my clothes-line, wondering what exactly that word meant, but too embarrassed to ask. My response was, "Yeah, but not even a phone call, Joey?"

He seemed to drift away then, as he always did when the subject of his mother arose. I intuitively knew to change the subject whenever he got that faraway sound in his voice.

He continued to ask me questions about what it was like to live in foster care or what it was like to have so many different parents. He wanted to know how I felt about my upbringing. Never before had any-one shown such passionate interest in me. It would be years before I realized that his assumed interest had little to do with me, and every-thing to do with his obsession with Marilyn.

After just one week he said he loved me, and he placed his gold chain with its football amulet around my neck. The football was Joey's most prized possession. It was from a prestigious boarding school in New Jersey, Lawrenceville, which had awarded him the medal for out-standing athletic ability in football. Joey said the talisman brought him luck. I would later learn that it was important to him because his father, the great Joltin' Joe, never came to see his football games or even acknowledged Joey's athletic abilities. For him, the amulet seemed to even out the score in some way. It proved to him that *somebody* believed in him. Although I didn't understand any of these nuances at the time, I knew the gold football was extraordinarily special. This amulet was his sign of commitment to me, and I felt honored.

I did a lot of thinking that week before deciding whether I would return home and obey my mother's new rules. I had less than three months until I graduated, and I was determined to finish. If I didn't graduate, I would disappoint my counselor, Mr. Cousineau. More than anything else, I wanted to see a smile on his face at my graduation. I wanted to repay Mr. Cousineau for his years of kindness and support.

Without calling, I simply walked back into my house one week after my disappearance. True to form, both my grandmother and my mother acted as if nothing out of the ordinary had happened. They seemed happy to see me. My mother turned off the television, which in itself was a miracle. As usual, Grandma offered me a cigarette, which I gladly took. The three of us began chatting like old friends as Grandma and I blew smoke rings, though this ritual was ordinarily done before the Jesus, Mary, and Joseph statues in the sanctuary of our bedroom.

Mother asked offhandedly, "Where have you been?"

"I stayed at Bobby's apartment a few nights and Sara's two nights. I took the bus to work, but I didn't go to school." This inaction didn't faze them in any way.

"I see," said Mother.

I added, "I also met a boy at the bowling alley, and I think I'm in love."

Now showing more interest, Mother continued, "Really? Tell us about him." Excited to have her undivided attention, I launched into a lengthy description of Joey. When I said "Joe DiMaggio" in the course of the conversation, you could have heard a pin drop. Stunned, they asked about his last name to make sure they had it right.

Mother asked if he was related to *the* Joe DiMaggio, the great ball player, to which I replied, "Who? What are you talking about?"

They patiently explained the history of this famous ball player and his celebrated marriage to Marilyn Monroe, and wondered if my new boyfriend was related to them.

"I don't know, but I'll ask him."

On the phone, I asked him, "Do you know anything about a famous ball player named Joe DiMaggio who was married to Marilyn Monroe?"

With a chuckle of delight in his voice, he said, "Yes, that would be my family. He's my father, and she was my stepmom."

Surprised that in all of our intimate conversations Joey never mentioned this to me, I weakly blurted, "Oh."

I wasn't sure how to process our conversation. It didn't make much of an impact on me until I reported this information to my mother and grandmother and pandemonium ensued. They were more than elated; you would have thought that I had just won the lottery.

My mother got up off the couch (which for some time was something she only did when visiting the bathroom or returning to her bed) and began to pace the living room floor as she pondered this new development. "Oh, my God, Dawn, this is fantastic! I've always told you that it's just as easy to fall in love with someone *with* money as it is with someone who's poor."

I shook my head, "Mom, Joey doesn't have any money. He just got out of the service and doesn't even have a job or a car yet."

Mother reasoned, "It makes no difference, Dawn, if he's got money or not; coming from the DiMaggio family is the same as having money."

Puzzled and exasperated, I said, "Mother, what are you talking about?" But by now, my mother had the faraway, dreamy look that she would get on her face when she was listening to "Who's Sorry Now?". Bewildered by this reaction, I grew silent.

I couldn't remember a time when such high spirits had filled our home. It was as if my mere association with Joey had forever changed *their* lives. Their excitement was contagious, and I felt a euphoric bliss.

A few days later, when Joey met my family, a mysterious love affair began among the three of *them*. Joey practically moved into my already-cramped house. Instead of job hunting, he spent his days talking with—charming, you might say—my mother and grandmother. Coming home from work or school, I often felt like the intruder interrupting a private family affair. I was the tolerated family member encroaching upon their lively, intimate conversations. I have absolutely no memory of what they talked about, but it was clear that the three of them had deeply bonded.

Within six weeks, Mother and Grandma were talking about the two of us getting married. They let Joey live with us while he was getting settled. I felt torn between my desperate desire to escape from my family and the exhilarated feeling of making my family happy at last. It felt as if I had found the Holy Grail, and I alone had the power to share it with my family or let it slip away. I did love Joey, but marriage? The thought panicked me. I was only seventeen, and I hardly knew him.

In the spring of 1963, some six months after Marilyn's death, Joey and I went to a movie simply called *Marilyn*. Having only dated for a couple of months, I still had a lot to learn about him. As soon as the movie started, there was a noticeable change in him. I could feel his entire body get smaller and smaller as he curled in on himself. I couldn't understand what was happening. Dry, tortured sobs emoted from his small, imploded frame. We were always affectionate with each other, so I reached out to soothe him, but he only pulled further into himself. It became obvious to me that he wanted to be alone with her. He seemed to float out of his body trying to merge with her image on the screen. It was eerie, and I felt totally alone. He was in a different world—a world he was creating for himself. I didn't know what to make of his behavior, much less what to do about it.

In subsequent days—years—I would come to understand how devastated Joey was by Marilyn's death. He was released early from the Marines due to psychological problems he never would discuss, which explained why he was adrift. He was lonely and depressed. Marilyn's death seemed to have exacerbated something deeply troubling in him, as if she had been the last tie to the family he barely knew.

Desperately wanting to move out without hurting my family and terrified of a marriage commitment, I felt frantic and utterly lost. One night I went out with a girlfriend and got drunk (a new behavior for me at that time). In my stupor, I boarded a bus for Los Angeles. I passed out on the bus and was eventually taken off by the police at the Los Angeles bus depot. Because I was a minor, I was taken to Juvenile Hall. Scared, humiliated, hungover, and obedient, I complied with everything I was directed to do by all concerned authorities.

They called my older brother, Ronnie—fresh out of the Marines and now working at Disneyland in nearby Anaheim. He picked me up at the detention center and brought my disheveled self to his apartment. He called our mother for advice on what to do next.

The next day, my mother sent Joey to fetch me. On the drive home from Los Angeles to San Diego, Joey pushed for marriage.

"Let's get married, Dawn, I love you and want to spend my life with you. We could kill two birds with one stone that way."

"What do you mean?" I said, suffering from my first horrific hangover.

"Well, I need a place to live and settle down, and you want to move away from your family. Let's just get married and get an apartment."

"Joey," I protested lamely, "I am only seventeen, and besides, I have to finish high school."

"We could get married now and stay with your family until you finish school in June. Then we could move to Los Angeles. There are lots of jobs in Los Angeles. Besides, you know that your mother and grandmother want us to get married, right? I am crazy about your family, Dawn, and we love each other. Why not get married?"

"I don't know, Joey, it all just seems so fast."

"Well, I see it as the solution to each of our problems."

Feeling weak, repentant, and without options, I consented to marriage.

When we returned to my house, I went directly to my room to sleep while Joey, my mother, and my grandmother happily planned our upcoming wedding. The scenario with my mother, grandmother, and Joey arranging our wedding is reminiscent of how Marilyn came to her first marriage to Jim Dougherty when she was sixteen. As widely reported, her marriage was contrived and agreed upon by Marilyn's foster mother, elderly aunt, and the Doughertys.

***

Marilyn and I were both compliant with these plans. We saw marriage as a way to escape our current problems, and must have had the misguided assumption that marriage equaled freedom. Gloria Steinem quotes Marilyn as saying, "Being married to Jim brought me escape at the time. It was that or being sent off to another foster care home . . ." There were few other options for women in our situation at that time, and we believed that we were simply following convention. All of the adults in both of our lives wanted us safely tucked away in the arms of marriage.

Back in the sixties, the institution of marriage was a legitimate way of keeping a girl safe. Or so it seemed.

A Virgin Sacrifice

IT WAS MAY 18, 1963 when Joey and I married, a few months after our first meeting. We were accompanied by my mother, blessings in tow, and our mutual friend, Tommy.

Joey wanted the wedding in a location where there would be no news coverage, so he decided on Winterhaven, California, a small agricultural town not far from Yuma, Arizona. None of the local media were notified, nor were most of our friends.

For reasons that were unclear to me, Joey had not even told his parents he was getting married. Now, as I reflect on Joey's life up until we met, I realize it must have been difficult to have spent his young life in a fish bowl. Eventually, I would come to see that practically every move he made was in the news. "Joe DiMaggio Jr., son of the great baseball player, Joe DiMaggio, visits his father," or "Young DiMaggio joins the Marines," or, "is beside his father at Marilyn's funeral." *My* Joey was an intensely private person. He did everything he could to minimize attention to himself, and he avoided any negative attention that could reflect objectionably toward his father.

I must have been in a haze the morning of our wedding, because I can't remember any of our drive from San Diego to Winterhaven. The trip was about one hundred and sixty-five miles of rocks and desert—boring enough to expect that conversations would have taken place, but nothing broke me out of my trance. I recall hugging my grandmother good-bye, and the next thing I was aware of was the Justice of the Peace saying, "I now pronounce you man and wife."

Suddenly, as if coming out of a coma, I awoke and glanced around the small chapel, recognizing Mother, Tommy, and this young man who was, apparently, my new husband. My first thought was, *This is just plain crazy; how come everyone is acting so happy? Oh my God, what have I done?*

We went through the expected pleasantries after the brief ceremony and took a few quick snapshots. I changed out of my borrowed, beautiful white dress and into my new blue culottes and multicolored blouse that tied at the waist. My mother had painstakingly juggled her carefully assembled envelopes of bills to dig up the money for me to have this lovely new outfit, along with a lacy nightgown. She wanted my wedding day and weekend honeymoon to be as special as she could make it.

Intoxicated by the wedding ambience, I too became excited and hopeful as our small group shared a quick lunch—and then Joey and I were off to begin our new life together. It seemed like only a snap of a finger, and just like that, I was a wife. As Joey pulled away from the curb, I leaned out of the window to wave good-bye to everyone. Smiling, I turned to face Joey, only to be met with a startling stone wall of silence. I blinked my eyes in puzzlement that he, by all appearances, didn't look happy. Wasn't he the one who wanted this marriage, and weren't we in love?

No words, no sounds, only deafening silence. Over the next four hours, as we drove to Los Angeles, it seemed as though a fierce tension was building within him. I was frozen in my seat, bewildered and frantically trying to understand what I had done to create this situation; that feeling would become a pattern that would manifest itself repeatedly during our tumultuous, on-again, off-again, two-year relationship. Years later, I would discover that Joey's father displayed this identical stone-walling behavior with Marilyn, withdrawing into silence for hours, or even days, at a time.

I came close to having a panic attack as I desperately tried to engage him in conversation. His silence prevailed. I wondered if he was mad at me, but I was too afraid to ask. I began to obsess about every aspect of that day: every word that I had said, everything I had done, and everything that I had worn. I replayed everything. I looked down to assess the blue pedal pushers, the blue-patterned shirt tied modestly at the waist. I wondered if I was too exposed. I didn't know yet that he *expected* a sexpot and *desired* exposure.

Noticing his hands were turning white as they gripped the steering wheel, I said, "Joey, wasn't that minister's shirt funny-looking?"

Silence! Overwhelming anxiety precluded my being quiet. "I couldn't believe my mom coughed so much during the wedding, did you notice?" On and on went my babbling, to be met by dead silence; not a single movement or sound came from him. His body, rigid as a stone, sat behind the steering wheel, staring straight ahead.

After a time I asked with forced cheerfulness, "Are you hungry, Honey?" Still, nothing. My fretfulness drove me to babble about a funny joke Tommy made at lunch, and any topic or action during the wedding I could recall. Finally, I fell into a rigid silence as well.

I wanted to reach out and touch his face or hold his hand, anything, but I was confused, lost, and immature. I was scared. I was wildly in love with my prince, even though I would have preferred to defer the marriage to some day in the future when I felt more ready for this giant step. But I would have done anything to see him smile. He remained frozen in his silence.

We stopped before dark at a Jack in the Box, my favorite place to eat. We didn't go inside, but ordered our food at the drive-through window. Back on the road, we ate our tacos and drank our Cokes in silence.

God in heaven, I wondered, *what is he thinking about?*

Just past dark, we checked into a motel room. I was dumbfounded when Joey went straight to bed. Tears were cascading down my cheeks as I peered down at the traffic from the tiny balcony overlooking the famous Sunset Boulevard. Adorned in the delicacy of my sheer, lacy nightgown, I replayed the day's events repeatedly, trying to understand what I had done to make my prince withdraw into his cold silence the moment the wedding was over. Since childhood I had visualized this night so many times. It was to be the most exciting night of my life. But now?

I had already given myself to him two weeks earlier in a cheap hotel in Los Angeles. Joey really wanted to have sex; I decided that even if he abandoned me afterwards, I would give in. I knew that many guys just left a girl after getting the sex they wanted, but I tried to consider that at least my first experience would be shared out of love. I was so scared and uptight, the experience was not enjoyable for either of us. What I recall about that night was the strained atmosphere before the sexual act and the mutual disappointment after. Nonetheless, Joey remained kind and loving to me in the days following, fostering my hope for our future.

***

My head was spinning with so many conflicting thoughts. I remembered all the years when life was literally in the dumps, and this was supposed to be the start of my new, wonderful, magical life. On this night, my wedding night, I had hoped to be twice redeemed. First, I would be redeemed from my trashy background, since I had remained a virgin until Joey. At least I had saved myself for my one true love—which is what all men want, right? A virgin! I had always heard that "the first time" was where men placed the highest value.

Joey hadn't said much about our first time in love's embrace, but I thought he would be proud of me since we were now married. He knew he had been the first man I had slept with. My second redemption would come from God's forgiveness for having had sex before marriage. Hadn't I rectified my mistake by marrying the man to whom I had given myself? God would forgive me. I was sure of it!

So his silence on that night made me feel like I was sitting in a courtroom waiting for a jury to decide my guilt or innocence. I was on my feet, pacing and waiting breathlessly with anticipation for my new husband's explanation of his attitude—and, more importantly, my ultimate state of reprieve. I sat shocked, mortified, confused, and ashamed as my bridegroom slept soundly.

The evening continued to pass slowly while party sounds from Sunset Boulevard drifted up toward my balcony. Feeling more alone and frightened than I could ever remember having been before, my stomach began to ache the way it always did whenever I tried to contain the thoughts and shame of my past—especially the feelings that threatened to pull the curtain off of my newly groomed façade of confidence.

Adding to my confusion was the soft caress of my nightgown against my skin, which brought feelings of longing, along with some kind of embarrassment. The tears trickling down felt like fire pricking at my hot cheeks. I was grateful for the pint of celebratory vodka I had stored in my suitcase, never dreaming I would be drinking it alone as I pondered my wedding night disaster. Sitting with my head in my hands, heartbroken at the state of affairs surrounding what should have been the happiest night of my life, I spent the night downing the vodka—straight—and gazing at a dark room.

Heartbroken, I believed that my carefully protected dowry was insufficient to please my husband, and not good enough to grant me the pardon that I had longed for. I could relate to an innocent prisoner who is granted a pardon. Having never committed the crime in the first place, what I really wanted was to be exonerated. I frantically wanted *something* from Joey. Acknowledging my virginity would have felt as if a priest were giving me absolution, a cleansing, a reprieve, a proof of sorts that I was a good person. I desperately needed to prove that I was unspoiled merchandise, worthy to walk with my head held up, if not high, at least at eye level with the world at large.

The next morning, I took his lead and acted as if nothing unusual had happened. I asked no questions since I was afraid of the possible answers. What if he said that he regretted marrying me? What would I do then? So off to breakfast we went, holding hands just like any other newlywed couple. Later in the day, we moved into our tiny apartment and the start of our new life.

***

A full week elapsed before lovemaking ensued. Then, a once-a-week-on-Sunday-only-because-I'm-obliged-to pattern emerged. These Sunday morning, disenchanted attempts at lovemaking would eventually be the undoing of our marriage. His impotency was never a problem for me. My difficulty resided in his accusations and misguided solutions. Unable to complete the sexual act, Joey would become furious with me. His blaming words accumulated like small bricks stacking themselves against my mind, body, and heart, building a wall. I had to accept most of this in silence. Naïve and inexperienced, I didn't know how to talk about the problem. I didn't know that the problem could be his, or at least ours, and not just mine alone.

He once said to me, "Having sex with you is like taking candy from a baby." I didn't know what he meant by that, and was too intimidated to ask. I just shut down, gradually withdrawing deeper into myself. With barely a thread of self-esteem to hang onto in the first place, I was confused and bewildered: there was scarcely a *me* to be found. I did not understand what it was he wanted or what it was that I was doing wrong, since I was always willing to participate. His anger would start right in the middle of the sexual act, when all of a sudden he would push himself away from me. He spent the rest of the day ignoring me or being verbally abusive.

I was in love, and I desperately wanted to please my new husband. Unfortunately, he seemed to want the one thing that I was the most incapable of giving him: a raw, strut-your-stuff-screw-your-brains-out sex-initiating-woman. Or at least, that's what he professed to want. We argued endlessly over his desire for me to wear sheer, Kleenex-thin, clingy jersey turtleneck-type shirts and the open cleavage-type blouses that would accentuate my breasts. I wanted to hide them behind as many layers of clothes that the California sunshine would comfortably allow.

In the beginning of our marriage, my social and sexual naiveté precluded any understanding of Joey's intended objective. I thought he married me because he loved me. I doubt that he was even conscious of the urgency of his intended makeover. Nevertheless, the intensity of his desire to mold me into the contour of Marilyn's image was heartbreaking. We fought often about the perfect female persona; in particular, mine versus Marilyn's.

I misinterpreted and underestimated his idealization of Marilyn. He told me many times of their close relationship, that he called her often to discuss any problems he was having, that, in fact, they had spoken the night of her tragic death. I assumed she was like a mother figure to him. I eventually came to understand that, from the time he first met her at the impressionable age of ten, he was deeply enthralled with Marilyn at a number of different levels, from nurturing to sexual.

Redemption, a pardon? Au contraire! Joey bargained for a provocative Marilyn, and what he got was a mere, unseasoned child. He was angry at the naiveté of my guarded virginity. My badge of honor now superfluous, he lent me penance by tying his impotence around my throat. Once again discarded, no redemption would be granted.

The Prince's Pauper Bride

CLASS CAN BE defined as rank, tribe, costume, grooming, culture, acculturation, education, manners, and taste. Class also includes attitudes and assumptions. It is an implicit and explicit source of identity.

Joey was as different from me as dark to light. He was upper class, eloquent, and always tastefully dressed. He was educated at the best schools available, including a short stint at Yale, while I was gratuitously passed with benefit of remedial classes by my high school. He was brilliant and articulate, while I stammered incomplete sentences and mispronounced basic words.

His table manners were impeccable. Once, at dinner, he delicately dissected an artichoke, a vegetable that I had never laid eyes on and would not have known how to begin to eat. I watched, mesmerized, as he drew each artichoke leaf through his teeth before placing the remains in a perfect circle around the edges of his hors d'oeuvre plate. I, on the other hand, less brave with the unfamiliar, would always eat something with the word "chicken" in the menu description. I was, after all, familiar with chickens. Unsure of which fork to use first, or where to place my napkin, I would just hold them in my hand until I saw how others managed these things.

He dressed in linen shirts, tailored slacks, and loafers with tassels. Lacking any degree of fashion sensibilities, I wore whatever ill-fitting outfits I had purchased from the Goodwill store. Throughout high school, I had mostly worn borrowed clothes from kind neighborhood girlfriends willing to share their wardrobe.

I don't think Joey really meant to look down on me, but one cannot be educated without eventually cringing at the mispronunciation of even simple words. I frequently said things like, "Joey, I don't got no clothes to wear."

Marilyn was reported to have said, "A man can't love a woman for whom he feels contempt," explaining, "He can't love her if his mind is ashamed of her."

I'm quite sure that, like myself, there were times when Marilyn wanted to shrivel up and hide from the assumptions, even jokes, about her purported "dumbness." She is also reported to have said: "I suddenly knew myself. How clumsy, empty, uncultured I was, a sullen orphan with a goose egg for a head."

She emphasized this belief in her last interview before her death—she begged reporters, "Please, don't make me a joke."

***

Shortly after our marriage, Joey introduced me to his cousin, Betty, and her husband, Bud. Betty was the daughter of Joe Sr.'s sister, Marie, with whom he was living in San Francisco. When I stepped into the foyer of Betty's home for the first time, my eyes got as wide as saucers. I was overwhelmed by the massive crystal chandelier and the large, winding staircase with shining wooden banisters. My inability to know how to behave was apparent. I was panicked by what I should do, might do, or might say, and my immediate reaction was to turn and hide in the restroom. The home itself alarmed me. How can one even think of stepping on such magnificent, flawless floors or sitting on such elegant furniture with a body that has never before done so?

Had it not been for the loving graciousness of Betty, I may never have come out of the bathroom. At dinner everyone had their own little sterling silver set of salt and pepper shakers. Then there was the silverware to contend with. I was a nervous wreck as I tried to secretly watch what everyone else did. I kept mixing things up and dropping the silverware. To make things worse, I stuttered. I always did this more when I was anxious, which further embarrassed Joey.

I tried to cover up my awkwardness by talking. I said to Betty, "Joey tells me that you just got back from a trip to Germany?"

Betty replied, "Yes, we just returned home last Sunday. It was a wonderful vacation."

"Oh, that sounds fabulous," I replied. "Have you ever been to Europe?" I saw everyone look at one another, but I didn't understand why. The sinking feeling in my stomach told me that I had just made a mistake, but I couldn't identify what it was. I had that old familiar sense that someone had opened a little door on the top of my head and was pouring a gallon of ice water through me. I felt mortified by the reaction in the room. Someone thankfully changed the subject, but I wanted to crawl under the table. Kind Betty tried to keep me in the conversation with more questions.

Betty said, "So, Dawn, Joey tells me that the two of you spent a weekend at my Uncle Joe's house in San Francisco, and that you had a little 'upset' with my mother, Marie."

I replied in my usual poor grammatical style, "Yes! I just thought that it was pretty weird that Marie wanted me and Joey to sleep in separate bedrooms since we'd got married already."

Betty replied, "Well, it's not weird if you know my mother, but that sure sounds like her Catholic righteousness stuff. Anything else about your visit with my Uncle Joe and my mother seem weird to you?"

"Well, it seemed kind of strange to me that so many things in the house had 'Joe DiMaggio' written on it. His name was on the table-cloths, the pillow cases, the bathroom towels, the kitchen towels, and even on the coffee cups and sugar bowl. Didn't he know his name already? Oh yeah, and the living room furniture all had little claw feet that reminded me of little animals. That was really strange. I never saw nothing like that before."

Joey rolled his eyes at my comments, and I could tell that he was getting irritated and that he wanted me to shut up. It wouldn't be long before I understood that a big part of his irritation was my profound ignorance on all topics, especially my poor grammar. In this case, he hated my ignorance regarding antique furniture, crystal, china, and other things presented to his father as gifts that were considered good taste in decorating.

Sweet Betty ignored the looks between Joey and Bud and continued engaging me. Gently chuckling, she explained, "That antique living room furniture is really ugly; it would scare the pants off a saint! When Marilyn lived in that house, she tried in vain to get my Uncle Joe to allow her to remodel the place, but Joe wouldn't have it. That's exactly the way the house looked when his parents were alive. Joe absolutely refused to change a single thing about it, which was a point of contention between him and Marilyn. I sure don't blame her for not wanting to live there. Uncle Joe and my mother keep that place like a shrine and it *is* truly depressing. But then, my mother is depressing, the way she makes Joe her whole life, like he's a king or something. She never did have much time for me when I was growing up, because everything was about her 'beloved famous brother, Joe.' *The* Joe DiMaggio. Why, she waits on him hand and foot, and it still makes me sick to think about it."

Betty's husband, Bud, rolled his eyes as he shook his head, then suggested with a big sigh, "C'mon, Joey, the 49ers are playing; let's go watch them."

I let out a long breath as Betty smiled warmly, lighting up another cigarette while offering me one as well. My shoulders slowly uncoiled away from my ears as I inhaled deeply. I smiled back at Betty as we began clearing the table. I thought how much I liked this lovely woman.

***

I didn't meet my mother-in-law, Dorothy Arnold, until Joey and I re-united after our first separation. For reasons that remained a mystery to me, he wanted nothing to do with his mother. As widely reported Joey went some fifteen years without seeing her. There was something really odd about their relationship. The only consistent relationship that he seemed willing to maintain was with his stepmother, Marilyn. So many things about his life were unknown to me, or would have been incomprehensible even if I had known then. Being immature and idealistic, I begged him to reconcile with his mother. Looking at me with amusement and resignation he said, "Deliver me from people who mean well." In retrospect, I should have left well enough alone.

I adored Dorothy. Shortly after we met, she began to call me "Baby Ducks." I loved the nickname, but then, I would have loved any name she chose. She mesmerized me. She was beautiful, eccentric, and—I'm sad to say—alcoholic. When she drank, which was most of the time, she could be loud and obnoxious. Other times she could charm your socks off with her showgirl-style seduction. She had been a showgirl and called herself an actress. According to her, she couldn't get any roles because the great Joe DiMaggio blackballed her in the movie industry.

I remember how she waltzed into our apartment, her platinum blond page boy hairstyle brushing against her Italian silk blouse, her pants of the finest linen. Always dramatic, she smoked cigarettes with a black and gold cigarette holder, adding to her grace and mystique.

I can only guess at my mother-in-law's impressions of me. I imagine she thought something like, "Oh my god, what has my son got himself into marrying this girl-child? She can hardly put a coherent sentence together. She dresses like she picked her clothes from a grabbag. And her hair is a fright. With her bleached blond, brassy locks she looks outdated and just plain poor. She gives the impression of some stray that my boy picked up along the way."

Dorothy was extremely conscious of people's opinions. Having been a showgirl and Joe DiMaggio's first wife, and having lived in the fast lane among the "beautiful" people, she personified everything that Hollywood represented.

To her credit she was always kind to me. She gently began teaching me how to tone down my hair color in a way that made me feel cared about instead of criticized. She gave me a couple of articles of clothing that were way too large but were still an improvement over my secondhand store items. She also taught me about the magic of wearing scarves to accent a piece of clothing.

"Hi Baby Ducks, I brought this new hair color today because I thought it would look beautiful with your skin color. Would it be okay if we tried it on you? I also brought this navy blue scarf, here, let me show you how to tie it around your neck."

I would have let her put the color orange on my hair if she had wanted. The combination of hair coloring coupled with smoking cigarettes seemed to me the most intimate kind of friendship between mothers and daughters. I therefore assumed an intimacy that actually never existed.

That year I got a job as a receptionist on Rodeo Drive in Beverly Hills. Seeing how lovely the women dressed, I asked for their fashion help. They took me under their wing and taught me about style, colors, textures and how to dress for success. Today I still use their tips, and remain grateful for their time and effort.

One event with Dorothy stands out in my memory. It was shortly after we met when she took Joey and me to dinner at the home of a couple of her good friends, Al and James, who were also in the motion picture business. In introducing us, Dorothy said, "Al, I'd like you to meet my new daughter-in-law, Baby Ducks—but you can call her Dawn." I glowed with pride at hearing my nickname.

Al took my hand in his, smiled warmly as he looked me directly in the eye, and said, "Welcome, my dear, I'm so pleased to meet you." It seemed like a personal invitation to some strange, new world.

I must have appeared like the pauper I was and behaved like one of the Beverly Hillbillies in the way I spoke. I was totally awed as I glanced around their magnificent home. Enthralling, soft music filtered through the air, and candles gave a glow and emanated a delightful fragrance. There was a velvety feel to the pure white, wall-to-wall carpet. The effects of the gorgeous furnishings in the room stunned me. My bare feet delighted in the soft, furry feeling of the carpet, but I could not take my eyes off the black mahogany piano. Although I had seen a piano up close before, I had never seen a baby grand. I held my breath at the sight of such beauty, the lines and curves of this magnificent thing. I wanted to touch it, to embrace it, to ingest its grandness. Instead, I stood frozen to the floor, unable to tear my longing eyes away. Al saw my fixation on the piano, perhaps even recognized that *something* was happening, because he gently took my arm and said, "Would you like to sit down over here by me and I'll play something for you?" All I could do was nod my head in consent.

Al played music just for me, while James fussed over drinks and dinner. Al's playing relaxed me, just like the moving leaves on the old eucalyptus trees used to soothe me years before. Our hosts didn't probe, and asked nothing of me all evening. I did not have to make "happy" conversations, terrified of making a mistake; I could feel their caring attitude. They just let me rest and be myself—which was so pleasantly relaxing in that atmosphere.

Like at Betty's house, the effect of such beauty was deeply moving for a girl who had spent weekends in dilapidated old trailers with taped-up windows and houses without paint or grass or beauty of any kind. It was like experiencing for the first time the intoxicating smell of those long-ago sweet peas.

Three or four years after my divorce from Joey, I visited California, and through the grape vine I heard that Dorothy was ill and that her alcoholism had greatly progressed. Unannounced, I drove to Palm Springs to visit her. She refused to see me. Crushed, I returned to San Diego. It would take a long time before I understood that just because someone offers you an olive branch of kindness does not mean that they feel or even desire any closeness in the relationship. In this case, I was once her daughter-in-law, and in her kindness she had done the best she could in accepting me. Anything else was merely a figment of my wishful imagination.

With a Name like DiMaggio

WINDOW SHOPPING ON Hollywood Boulevard became our weekend entertainment ritual. Money was scarce, as it often is for newlyweds. Joey worked sometimes as a day laborer, and I worked as a bank file clerk. He had little contact with his father, but would not have taken money from him even if it had been offered. Joey was a prideful young man in those early days, and would have starved before he asked for help from his famous father.

I had just turned eighteen in the summer of 1963 when I first met the great Joe DiMaggio Sr. The intrigue and behavior surrounding that first meeting resembled a scene straight out of a gangster movie. After picking up Joey at our apartment, the driver and some friends drove my new father-in-law over to meet me in front of my bank building at twelve noon sharp.

Feeling nervous in anticipation, and wanting to make a good impression on Joey's father, I could hardly concentrate on filing ledger sheets at the bank that morning. I was dressed in my fancy, Goodwill pink-and-white-checkered seersucker suit and wearing my only pair of heels. I had even purchased a new pair of stockings especially for the occasion.

At exactly twelve noon I stepped outside of the bank and into the bright sunshine, where Joey, his father, and three other very tall men—all dressed in ties, dark suits, and sunglasses—were waiting for me. We politely shook hands, and the six of us walked to a nearby restaurant. It was dark inside the restaurant, and Joe Sr. sat as far away from me as the seats allowed, as if he had planned it that way. No one spoke to me throughout the entire meal, although a couple of the men would send a nod or smile my way throughout lunch to at least acknowledge my presence. But Joe Sr. barely even spoke with his son, who for the most part remained silent, speaking only a word or two with the other gentlemen seated at the table.

Joey was always ill at ease at these infrequent gatherings, as if intensely calculating the precise moment to inject his two cents into the conversation. He was ever-so-mindful to be abreast of every sporting event imaginable as if he might be given an impromptu test. The tension in my husband was palpable. I was unaccustomed to this side of him, since I had always seen him as being completely self-assured and confident.

I would eventually realize that Joe Sr. would never want to have a meal with just the two of us, nor would he ever want to set foot in our apartment, as if it would taint his reputation. I came to realize that it was somehow beneath him. We were always chauffeured to our meetings in a large black limousine. One of his cronies would meet us at our door before escorting us to the car, where Joe Sr. was waiting. I remember having a couple of dinners in the company of George Raft (best known for his role in the movie *Scarface*) and Willie Shoemaker (known as the most successful jockey in history). Mr. Shoemaker was one of the nicest men I ever met; he went out of his way to be kind to me. At that time, I had never heard of either of them, which everyone but Joey found amusing.

As I would soon learn, the only acceptable topics of conversation were sports, weather, and food—pretty much in that order. My presence was as insignificant as if I were one of the place mats on the table. I suppose Joe Sr. did at least notice me, however, since—according to Joey—he told Joey that I looked a lot like Marilyn after our first meeting. I have no way of knowing if this was true, but I wondered years later if his father's comment had anything to do with Joey's increased attention to the way I dressed.

Shortly after that first meeting, Joey's urgency toward managing my manner of dress seemed to increase. While window shopping, he would remark, "Look at that blouse, you would look great in that. That's how Marilyn would have dressed."

I'd reply, "Oh my God, Honey, I could never wear something like that. Look at how low cut it is. My boobs would hang out."

His observation was, "That's the point, Sweetie, that's what men like to see. You have to do something about your clothing; you dress like some dowdy schoolteacher. You always look so gray and unsexy."

With pleading eyes and voice, I offered, "But, Joey, I'd die if men stared at me that way, thinking I was showing off, or that I was inviting them to stare at my breasts. Besides, why would you want other men to ogle me, anyway?"

In a voice dripping with contempt, he argued, "Dawn, you are so stupid. That's just how real women dress. They dress to please men, not hide from men. What's the matter with you? I've been around, and know how men are. You know nothing about what men want in a woman. Besides, do you think you know better than Marilyn?"

Hanging my head in embarrassment, I remained silent and considered his words. I knew that he was right about my not knowing anything, but it hurt so much that he wanted me to expose myself. For the life of me, I could not understand why he would want this. He was always talking about my shyness and sexual ineptness being the basis for our miserable sex life. I so wanted to please him in every way, but I couldn't make myself dress in such a provocative manner. I thought his request was like asking someone terrified of heights to stand out on a twenty-story scaffold to prove their love for him.

His constant disappointment made me feel like I was the one responsible for our disastrous bedroom trysts. I turned away from him so he wouldn't see my face burning with shame as I considered the miserable situation surrounding our sex life. There were facets of our sex life that frightened me. I could only guess at what the normal methods of satisfying a partner were. I tried to take my cues from Joey, thinking that since he was so worldly in matters of education, manners, and clothing, he would also know all there was to know about sex.

When Joey insisted on inserting a Coke bottle inside of me, I felt panic and disgust. I resorted to familiar childhood measures of survival by going limp and focusing on anything outside of the bedroom. This led to arguments and disappointments, as his sexual fantasies were thwarted by that behavior. In the absence of communication, all that remain are actions and reactions.

In the beginning, I was very responsive to his delicious, tender kisses, and shared in the explorations of our bodies. As time went on, however, his inability to maintain an erection occurred with more frequency. As I became more subject to his sexual fantasies, I further withdrew, flashing back to childhood memories of unwanted touching. As the months passed, the dreaded bedroom erection scenario happened almost every time we tried to make love.

Joey and I began to argue more frequently about my conservative attire. He forgot that I was the girl that had to repeat Physical Education classes because I refused to participate in group showers. As changing my manner of dressing became his solution to our sexual problems, I felt his urgency accelerate. He thought that if I dressed and behaved in a provocative manner, he would be aroused. I wanted with all my heart to please him, but my fear of being noticed sexually far exceeded his wishes for me to emulate Marilyn's dress style. We constantly fought about this. He made it clear that a normal woman would have known what *it* was that he was talking about, but between his fantasies and his need to be excited by showing off my body, I grew more and more frustrated. He said, "All *real* women already know about whoring." He said that as if every other woman on the planet besides me just woke up one morning and *voilà*, they instantly knew how to be a sexually provocative partner.

***

Shortly after my eighteenth birthday, my mother made the three-hour drive from San Diego to Hollywood to visit with me. The moment she sat down, I blurted out our bedroom difficulties. To my disbelief, she stood up and walked out of my apartment without a word. Weeping, I felt utterly alone and desperate in my bewilderment. It didn't help that my mother thought me unattractive. At least at that time she usually had *some* kind of advice—whether it was appropriate or not—and now she wouldn't even talk to me. I wondered if she blamed me for the sexual problems that I had just confided to her. Maybe she thought our sexual problems were because I was not pretty enough. I was so lost. "Why," I asked God, "do I seem to disappoint everyone in my life?"

As fall of 1963 approached, Joey and I moved from the Hollywood apartment we had been living in for about four months to Van Nuys in the San Fernando Valley. We had a larger apartment now, and our lack of furniture was more apparent. The bedroom had a box spring and mattress sitting directly on the floor, and we used stacked milk crates as dressers for our clothes. In the living room, we had two plastic pool chairs and an old television set sitting atop a wooden box. A card table was our dining room table. Our financial scarcity didn't bother me in the slightest, but our lack of intimacy did.

***

There was one event that captures, as well as summarizes, Joey's relationship with his parents, and it was quite mysterious to me. While I was at work, a falling steel joist hit Joey, causing an injury to his leg that required a massive amount of stitches. I was surprised that during his initial, weeklong hospital stay his father never came to visit him.

Once back home, Joey called his mother to help him bathe. It happened to be the same day I was temporarily laid off from my job, and returned home early in the afternoon. As I entered our tiny efficiency apartment, I heard laughter and water splashing in the bathroom. A sense of panic came over me as I quietly backed out of the door. *Oh my God*, I thought, *his mother is in there bathing him.* I kept asking myself, "If I had a father, would I allow him to help me bathe?" I wondered why Joey hadn't asked *me* to help him. What did this connection with his mother mean? What was I missing about their relationship? Why did I feel so weird? And why did my stomach hurt?

Everything seemed upside down and senseless. I spent the rest of the afternoon wandering around the neighborhood, afraid to return home.

***

Our situation further deteriorated as I began to notice Joey regurgitating and rechewing his food while holding his penis. During these times, he would refer to me as "Mommy." He would say in a child's voice, "Mommy, would you bring me a glass of water, please?" Without directly speaking to the problem, which I couldn't comprehend in the first place, I would skirt the issue by referring to any unpleasant situation as "our problem."

At some point I began pleading with him, "Joey, we need help. I don't know what's wrong with us, but something is, and we need help with our problem. Please come with me to counseling. I've seen this counseling stuff advertised, and it's supposed to help couples. I don't want to leave you, Baby, but I can't stand what's happening to us. Please, please come with me for help."

Once more, rather mindlessly, he answered, "We'll see."

After he ignored my pleas multiple times, I uncharacteristically gave him an ultimatum: "I'll wait one month for your decision. I can't go on like this, Joey. I will leave our marriage if you won't come with me to get help."

Ultimatum ignored, I left our marriage, brokenhearted. I came home early from work on a Friday afternoon and, enlisting the help of a girlfriend, I packed my things and was leaving when Joey and his friend came, tires screeching, into the parking lot.

His large, body-builder veins bulged out of his neck as Joey yelled at me, "You better not have the TV in that car! Do you hear me?" I was scared to death; I had seen the force of his temper many times when he slammed his fists into a wall.

I lied, "No, just my clothes and stuff." Mortified that he was more concerned about the TV than about my leaving, I wept.

I stayed with a co-worker for a few weeks. In those days, you had to have a substantial reason for a divorce. I requested that Joey file for the divorce, that way I would not have to say anything bad about him publicly that would end up in the papers. I only wanted my maiden name back. By now I had become as paranoid as Joey about protecting his father's name. Joey filed on the grounds that I badgered him for working too hard. That was funny, since I was the only one consistently working during our marriage, but it was an innocuous charge, so I agreed.

It seems odd to me now, but we spent a loving and tender evening together the night before he went to court for the hearing of the interlocutory decree. We cried in one another's arms, but still he refused to accompany me for professional help. It seemed as if his entire existence was focused on protecting the DiMaggio name.

In early spring of 1964, when we had been married just short of one year, our interlocutory decree was granted. To Joey's dismay, the press was there to cover the court hearing. Words were thrown, and then fists were thrown, between Joey and a news reporter. The *Los Angeles Times* headline read, "Young DiMaggio Clashes with Press." After he called me at work to tell me what happened, embarrassed, I rashly quit my job and moved to Santa Barbara. Sobbing, I gathered up my few things, threw them into our old Volkswagen, and drove like I was on fire.

This pattern of running away in the face of adversity had become my best coping skill, besides alcohol.

Joey continued to call me frequently. Within a month's time, he was commuting back and forth from Los Angeles to Santa Barbara as we continued to see each other. Whatever sexual problems we had had miraculously disappeared. There were no fireworks, mind you—there had never been fireworks between us—but our lovemaking was more sweet and tender. Still deeply in love with him, and without the sophistication to question the disappearance of his impotency, I happily moved back to Los Angeles to resume our marriage.

We were technically in violation of the court's interlocutory period by living together, but the most important part of this new arrangement was that we were together. Immediately, the impotency started again, and we were right back to square one with the same problem. I was mystified and devastated.

Lounging on the pull-out Murphy bed, this Sunday began like every other Sunday morning since I had reunited with Joey. Newspaper sections spread out everywhere, our half-empty glasses of orange juice sat on the floor next to the bed. The smell that came from the old mattress disgusted me. I wondered if this was due to its being closed up in the wall each day after we slept on it, or if the smell was embedded into the mattress from years of people doing what we were about to do. Either way, the thought and odor sickened me.

The ticking sound of the clock grew louder with every passing minute—or was it just the roar of my ticking insides? I noticed my hands shaking a little as I tried to concentrate on the newspaper. Please God, let this time be different. Please, God! Yet, in my heart, I knew we would replay the identical scenario that occurred every Sunday. Joey had just finished the sports section, so I knew that our ritual was about to begin. My heart pounded in worried anticipation as he gently lay on top of me. Within thirty seconds I knew we were headed for another troubled Sunday.

"God damn it," he exclaimed, "You moved!"

Instantly ashamed and contrite, I said, "Oh Joy, I am so sorry Honey, I was just trying to get comfortable."

"Yeah, well, you are always trying to get comfortable or some other damn thing, why can't you get this right?"

"I don't know, Joey, I am trying. I'll try and lay more still next time, ok?"

Shoving the covers aside, my young husband leaped out of bed and angrily stepped into his underwear. Slamming his right fist into the living room wall, he exclaimed once again, "God damn it! God damn it!"

Shriveled by his threatening anger, tears sliding down my cheeks, I turned on my side, knowing that he would punish me with silence for the rest of the day. I wondered which I dreaded more, his anger or his protracted silences. His silence reminded me of how my mother had behaved toward me when I was young. Entering her darkened bedroom to see if she needed anything, I was frequently met with brutal silence and eyes of steel. She scared me then, and Joey scared me now.

Struggling to control my sobs, I stuffed the corner of the pillow into my mouth like when I was a kid to avoid being heard. I knew with certainty that far worse things than yelling or wall-hitting can happen if cries are overheard. Once anger is loosed into a room, it has the potential of exploding into words that can slash the heart with gashes just as deep and as painful as physical blows to the flesh. I gagged as the Murphy bed smells threatened to overwhelm me.

I thought back to our dating days and how tingly I would become just thinking about Joey's kisses. Then, I couldn't wait until we could "legally" make love. How come I had those feelings then and not now? No, wait! That same feeling had also happened during our separation. The same butterflies in my stomach, and the same excited feeling, on those wonderful, clandestine afternoons when my housemates were gone and Joey and I had to hurry and make love before anyone got home. What had happened? Did I change? Did he change? How did we get here again? What was I doing wrong? Why couldn't he tell me? Wishing I knew how to ask him what the other *real* women knew, I wondered what he meant when he said that having sex with me was like taking candy from a baby. What does it mean to take candy away from a baby? Maybe it means it would be too easy? So does that mean he wants me to fight him off and not be so easy? Well that can't be right, because then I would have to move my body, which really makes him mad. So which is better, I wondered, to move my body or not to move my body? What was the right thing to do during sex? I was lost in a maze of self-doubt and confusion.

***

During this time, I tried to confide in Dorothy, my mother-in-law, about our troubles. In my naiveté, I thought that she and I had developed a close relationship

"Dorothy, I've heard about something called counseling where people can go when they're having troubles with their relationship or their families. I thought that would be a really good thing to help Joey and me."

To my disappointment and surprise, she replied, "With a name like DiMaggio, you cannot even think about such a thing. If any of this got out, it would be the end of all of us. Plus, his father would be furious." I kept asking myself why. I didn't know a thing about psychology, but I did wonder, after the bath incident, if she was afraid something would surface about her relationship with her son.

At that moment, I felt exactly the way that I had felt so many times in my life when I would say something seriously monumental, like, "Mom, just before Uncle Bill committed suicide, he tried to molest me," only to be met with skeptical stares as if I were the crazy person. When I was little, I couldn't understand the reasoning behind the actions of adults. Now that I was an adult, I still couldn't fathom why people reacted the way they did. Nothing made sense to me. Nothing!

After a few more months of failed sexual attempts, angry arguments, and constant remarks from Joey like, "You're beautiful, Baby, but could you just keep your mouth shut so people won't hear how dumb you really are?" I left our marriage even more devastated than the first time.

***

No one could have predicted that thirty-five years later, this prideful young man would be living in a junkyard in northern California, toothless, sporting a long gray, ponytail, and talking publicly about his father in a television interview with *Inside Edition*—his first paid interview! Perhaps his need for money to support his drug addiction outweighed Joey's pride or any sense of family secrecy. I can relate to that raw depth of degradation. The force called addiction possesses the soul, and it will supercede pride and self-respect in every area of one's life.

I loved Joey the way that only an eighteen year old heart can love, with every part of it and keeping nothing for itself. Oh God, how I didn't want to leave him. Yet I knew that I couldn't stay. Somehow, I understood that we would have destroyed one another.

It seemed to me that for my entire life there had always been an ominous *something* hanging in the shadows that I could never quite get ahead of, and I had been running from it for as long as I could remember.

Finding Out What "Real" Women Know

OK, JOEY, YOU want whoring, I'll learn whoring. Determined to become a "real" woman like he wanted, I moved into a new phase, one in which angry, indiscriminate dating abounded. My daily protocol included alcohol. Blackouts were scary, but permitted the depersonalization of every Tom, Dick, and Harry. I would definitely show my prince that I knew about whoring.

***

As far as I was concerned, I had kept my end of the bargain regarding morals and my impressions of God's ideas of purity. I had remained chaste despite an assumption of promiscuity from people who thought they knew something else about me. From my immature spiritual perspective, I wondered why I was being punished by God now by losing my marriage. I also wondered why I was being punished by Joey for something that I had always considered good: my sexual innocence. Once again, I raised my fist to the God that I had once loved. My feelings of loss, anger, and confusion were subdued by the blessed escape now provided by different *kinds* of spirits, like liquor.

It would be many years and a lot of therapy before I understood that I did not have sex *with* men, I had sex *at* them—or, to be more precise, *at* Joey. I avenged my internal rage at God, Joey, and men in general through promiscuity the same way that some people would cut on themselves in an effort to relieve their pain. Men became my self-flagellation weapon of choice. I used them as props, as carelessly as disposable paper towels, to fulfill some warped plan of revenge that drove me close to the edge of total self-destruction. My frustration and helplessness about the injustice of my plight became intolerable and with no recourse it turned to rage. I had to have a man in my life to be acceptable and yet being with a man would leave me feeling powerless and seething, without relief.

Alcohol became my new comforter, although I couldn't understand why I was unable to control my drinking once I took the first drink. I promised myself over and over that I would drink less the next time. After a night of drinking, I always thought I would do better *next time*. I believed alcohol was the solution to my increasing anxiety, never suspecting that alcohol *itself* had become my next problem. But drinking temporarily calmed my daily turmoil down to a manageable level.

Sometimes, after I had sex with a faceless body I would either feel like vomiting or doing myself bodily harm. Alcohol made my promiscuity bearable.

With the courage I derived from booze, I was determined to prove my "womanliness" to Joey. Though we were technically separated, he would hide in the bushes outside my apartment several nights each week, scaring the crap out of my dates when they brought me home. I missed my husband, and loved that he came by to sleep with me even though we weren't having sex.

Just home after a miserable date with another Hollywood "Mr. I-am-so-gorgeous-and-you-are-so-lucky-to-be-seen-with-me," I undressed and crawled into bed. The doorbell rang; the clock said 1:00 a.m. I knew who it was. Without a thought, I opened the door, Joey walked in, and he nodded an expressionless greeting as I turned and went back to bed. In the dark, I heard him undress. He crawled in next to me, and, without saying a word, he turned on his side and fell asleep. I felt relieved. At least this time he came over after my date had left so an embarrassing scene was avoided.

I stared at the ceiling as the hands on the clock marched toward morning and my new receptionist job on Rodeo Drive. I was trying hard to fit into the fast-paced Beverly Hills scene. It was the mid-six-ties—a culture of drugs, sex, and rock and roll. Hard as I tried, I was light-years out of my league. I was scared, tired, and frantic; like that *something* was relentlessly chasing me. I was tired of being tired. This peculiar visitation ritual of Joey's did not help. I wondered why he did it, but did I ever ask him why? No, of course not. I never asked questions of anyone. "Ignorance through silence" was the mantra I used to get by life's hardships. I had learned that lesson well, even though it was the cause of most of my problems. It always seemed that if I could ignore it, whatever bad was happening would go away.

***

I tried to hold my own among Hollywood's beautiful people. Fast cars, easy divorces, open sexual practices, rows of cocaine strung across expensive glass coffee tables—excess galore. I remember one evening in particular at a famous restaurant, The Luau, I was using a fake ID pro-claiming my age to be twenty-one and was drinking with the "beautiful people." Someone asked if I wanted to go to an orgy. Already a little drunk, I answered, "Sure."

A woman sitting at the table looked at me with alarm, "Dawn, you don't want to go to that party."

Defiantly, I stated, "Yes I do."

She said, "Do you even know what an o-r-g-y is?"

"Of course I know what that is." I acted offended that she would think me so stupid. Boldly sticking my chin out, I added, "Besides, I can take care of myself."

I do recall that concerned lady tried very hard to talk me out of going. I honestly thought that an orgy was simply a wild, drunken party. I had no idea what I was getting myself into. Without paying a bit of attention to my surroundings, off I went with a car full of strangers to a house located somewhere in the hills of Hollywood.

Once inside the house, after my eyes adjusted to the dim lighting, I noticed the living room, which was large and beautifully furnished. I became apprehensive seeing the perfectly laid-out lines of pure, white cocaine abundantly displayed on top of the glass coffee table. This was the mid-sixties, after all, when doing drugs was considered a chic thing to do; but I had grown up very close to the Mexican border, and I'd heard many horror stories of people dying of drug overdoses. I was much too frightened by those rumors to have experimented.

Bewildered by the open front door yet an absence of people, I began to search for a bathroom, but accidentally opened a bedroom door. The first thing that my eyes focused on was one of those lavender-colored lava lights with blobs of stuff dancing around inside the fluorescent liquid. Those lights were frightening—it was like watching little ghost bodies without eyes appear then shape-shift into even weirder ghost bodies, only to disappear again into another weird shape.

The nauseating smell of sweat and body fluids assaulted my senses as I focused on a number of undulating, nude bodies entwined upon a huge bed. I was frozen to the spot like a zombie, totally shocked at what was happening. I was wondering why these people were all together, doing whatever it was that they were doing. If they wanted to have sex, which was fine with me, why didn't each couple find their own bedroom? Out of the darkness, a man was walking toward me with the largest erect penis that I had ever seen in my life. I remember thinking, *My God, what is that, what does he do with that, what can he do with that,* followed by, *Oh, man, that thing must hurt!*

Squeezing my left breast, he said, "Hey, Baby, get those clothes off and join us," while he continued to walk past me to the bathroom. I was so petrified by this time that I peed a little in my pants. *I have to get out of this house.* The main problem was that I didn't know where I was or how to tell a cab where to pick me up.

Most normal people, at this point, would simply ask for the house address. Not me! Asking for directions was the furthest thing from my mind; I was sure that I was in the presence of rapists, or even murderers. I was *not* about to ask Mr. Naked Penis for directions. I wasn't totally crazy after all, just a bit misguided in the assessment of my ability to handle the situation. I was able to sneak into the bathroom, after which I went back to the living room and did what any brave, logical adult would do: I hid behind a recliner until sunrise.

For the rest of the evening, I was as quiet as a mouse as I listened to grunts, groans, and hollow, hilarious laughter mixed with various sounds that were unidentifiable. When naked people—I could see their reflection in the dining room glass door—came into the living room for another line of cocaine, I made myself into an even smaller ball behind the large leather recliner. I was scared that if they found me, they would grab me, pull me into the bedroom, and rape me.

As soon as I could see daylight, I quietly left my hiding place, ran to the nearest intersection that had street signs, returned to the house of undulating killers, and called a cab. Giving the intersection as the meeting place, I waited for what seemed like an eternity until the cab picked me up. I was covered with early-morning mist, and was hungry, scared, and terribly hungover.

When I gave the cab driver my address, he said with sharp disdain, "That will be twenty-five dollars, young lady."

I told him that I did not have that much money with me, but I could give him a personal check. With a contemptuous nod, he drove me to a grocery store parking lot and waited, with the meter running, until the store opened and I could cash my check.

I couldn't blame the man. After all, I must have been quite a sight, with smeared mascara from crying half of the night and the smell of pee wafting from my wrinkled clothes. I was just grateful to get home unmolested. Looking back, those people were probably safe enough; it was me who was way out of my league and didn't understand their language. At least their sexual agenda was right up-front and center (some more up-front than others).

Another example of my fear of exposure and inability to ask for help occurred while I was a guest on the boat of Max Baer Jr., who starred in the TV sitcom *The Beverly Hillbillies.* Max, along with my date, David, and I, left early one Saturday morning for Catalina Island.

After docking at the marina and rapidly consuming several cans of beer, I needed to use the restroom. I was unfamiliar with boat toilets, or as they called them, "heads." I couldn't figure out how to flush. Spying a small window high above the toilet, I got the bright idea of making a package of poop wrapped inside mounds of toilet paper. Package in hand, I stood on the toilet rim and tossed the contents out of the little porthole window while closing my eyes and hoping for the best. Once again, I suppose a normal person would have just stuck their head out of the bathroom door and asked something like, "Hey, how do you flush this toilet?" Not me! Oh no, no way. Too mortified to have asked such a question, I knew about the "Don't ask, don't tell" rule long before it was made popular by our military.

Thinking that I had handled the situation, one can imagine my horror as I went topside and saw my carefully wrapped package lying inside the dinghy that was tied up alongside the boat. A piece of the toilet paper was now waving in the wind as if mocking me. Without a lick of good sense, fully dressed, I jumped into the water from the top deck and disposed of the package before anyone noticed. Barely able to swim, I was fortunate to have survived that stunt.

Early that afternoon, somewhat dried off, walking hand in hand with my date, we headed straight to a fashionably noisy bar. I desperately needed a drink. After chugging down a few, Max and I became engaged in what we thought was an extremely meaningful conversation, the likes of which can only be produced by the effects of alcohol. We crawled underneath the table (understand, he was a really big guy), pulling the tablecloth down around us so we could finish our lifechanging conversation in peace and quiet.

Numerous insane episodes of this nature continued for three or four months while I continued drinking without interruption. Many of these incidents were humorous, but my naiveté and inability to read Hollywood body language only served to make things darker for me, which led up to one of the most traumatic experiences of my life.

Like a Bundle of Dirty Laundry

ONE AFTERNOON, WHEN I was buying a pair of shoes, I flirted with a cute shoe salesman. Slight of build, with blond hair and deep dimples, he seemed funny and engaging. After he insisted that I try on nearly every pair of shoes in the store, I finally left with a pair of shoes I could afford and a date that very evening. We both loved to jitterbug and there was a great band that night at a local nightclub. He was to pick me up, and dancing we would go.

My date rang the doorbell promptly at eight. He was a perfect gentleman in opening the car door for me and being attentive throughout the evening. We had such fun as we danced the night away. Both a little drunk, we left one club and decided that we would drop into a similar dance club nearby. First, he wanted to stop by his apartment to pick up his sport jacket. Fortified with alcohol, and without a care in the world, I followed him up to his apartment when he insisted I see the new and unusual fish he had just purchased. I wasn't into fish, but what the hell? I giggled a little sloppily as I stepped into his apartment.

Once inside, the fear I felt was instant and surprising—almost sobering—when I heard the locks click shut on his door. I heard three loud clicks, which immediately registered in my brain as odd since we were supposed to leave after fish-gazing and jacket-fetching.

Before I knew what was happening, I was body slammed against the wall. My head snapped back against the wall, then bounced forward into his face, which made him angry.

"You filthy slut!"

"Wa . . . wa . . . wait a minute."

"Shut your goddamn mouth, you whore!"

"Wait, please, what are you doing?" I said as he kissed—no, bit—into my lips.

Then I heard my skirt rip as he pushed and pulled me into the bedroom, slugging me in my arms, back and stomach. I was terrified by the sudden change in this man—from a regular guy into an animal. I couldn't make any sense of what was happening. I had difficulty deciding what would be my best course of action under the circumstances. By now, he had pulled and torn most of my clothes off and slammed me on his bed, which smelled like a filthy gym bag. I tried not to gag. I tried to think. I begged.

"Please stop. Please, you don't have to do this."

"I told you to shut your mouth, you cunt!" He slapped me hard across the face, then punched me in the stomach, but much harder this time.

"Keep fighting me, you little bastard, and I'll show you who's in charge here."

Once I fully realized that he would increase his violence the more I struggled, I stopped resisting and started focusing on how to get through what was happening. If I knew anything in life by now, I knew how to "just get through."

Then, silence and fucking. Hard, angry, brutal fucking. His sweat and gym bag smell dripping on my face.

"Please, please just finish."

"Shut up, you worthless piece of trash." It seemed that hours passed. Finally, unable to have an orgasm, he rolled off me and with contempt ordered, "Get dressed, slut."

I could hardly move, I was so sore, but I managed to piece together my torn clothes while a thick, blessed fog began to engulf me.

Just beneath the thick fog in my head was a scorching shame. I wondered how he could have known about my past and my recent experimentation, having just met me. I had known some of these truths about myself since *forever*: the stain of being a bastard child, the condemning words about me when the lady next door saw her husband touching me and shouted to the whole neighborhood what a filthy little slut I was. I felt encased in that proclamation of filth, which in my mind had just been proven true by a stranger. While this connection may seem outlandish, the feeling was overwhelming. The stain on me was indelible.

Finally, beneath the cover of darkness, the rapist dropped me off in front of my building. Reaching across me, he opened the car door and gave me a shove out of his car like I was a bundle of dirty laundry.

The dictionary says that rape is an outrageous violation.

My body was bruised from the rapist's fists, and my vagina was raw and torn from his prolonged inability to complete his act. Yet it was not the black and blue marks covering my body that left my spirit broken by his outrageous violation—it was his words. While the bodily harm from a physical battering imparts certain degrees of pain, they are temporary. Without question, the mental battering from an event so brutal brought alive a lifetime of psychological stabs and jabs that had worn me down. Skinless!

My shame had been sheathed, like it was in a snake's skin. So how could my rapist have known? Now, at home, his familiar, filthy words reverberated in my head, causing me to vomit again and again.

I considered the state of my body: outwardly bruised, but inwardly bleeding the bile from my history of indignity. Begging for immediate relief, I bathed in iodine. My skin was raw where I scrubbed myself with a Brillo pad to grind away all vestiges of my immersion in filth. I wrapped a raincoat around myself before choking down handfuls of Valium my mother had sent me from her stash. The Valiums were tiny little pills, yet each handful felt like shards of glass as they went down my throat. Now, finally, it would be finished.

I didn't think I could ever look anyone in the eye again as long as I lived. If this man knew the truth about me—that I was born a bastard and became a slut—then obviously everyone must know those things, too. The shame currently surfacing, along with my increasing self-hatred, was more than I could bear. I absolutely believed I had deserved the rape. After all, I had accepted the date, danced, and even had fun—just like when, as a child, I had taken the candy in exchange for touching. Didn't he, my rapist, say as much?

I went to the kitchen and lay down on the kitchen floor beneath a hissing gas stove. There was no suicide note; I had nothing to say to anyone. I was simply done. I closed my eyes and mercifully fell asleep.

Bam! All of a sudden, I woke with a start to the hissing sound of the gas the stove was emitting. Fighting to overcome the thick, foul smell of gas that hung in the air, I jumped up and opened a window. My lungs sucked the clean air in. The hands on the clock indicated a full hour had passed since I'd fallen asleep. My head throbbed. I turned off the gas and phoned my husband. "Joey, Joey, I've done something really bad. Please come right away. Please." Compelled by the urgency in my voice, he rushed over.

I opened the locked door at the sound of Joey's pounding. He walked passed me without a word. His face was tense and dark with rage. I sat back down on the couch and pulled a pillow close to my chest. Now I felt scared of him. "What the hell happened to you?" he shouted.

"I was beaten and raped by a man tonight."

Understandably angry that I let this happen to me, his anger at me for getting into this situation paled next to his rage at my perpetrator. Yet his commitment to preserving the family image obligated him to refuse to call the police. He was adamant that he did not want any press coverage.

Standing rigidly before me, with his hands on his hips, I felt as if he were going to hit me. "What in the hell were you thinking, going to sleep in front of that gas stove? You could have died, Dawn."

I weakly replied, "That was the point, Joey, that man hurt me bad."

"That's just plain crazy talk. So what if he hurt you, you're still alive, aren't you? You know we can't call the police! Do you want this to be all over the newspapers, the same way it was with Marilyn's death?"

"I'm just a nobody, Joey, why would anyone want to write about what happened to me?"

He shouted, "God, you are *so* dumb. It would be all over the papers because you're Joe DiMaggio's daughter-in-law. No police, and that's final! Do you understand me? I'm driving you down to your mother's house right now. Besides, you shouldn't have gone to that guy's apartment. You caused this mess in the first place. Now snap out of it and get packed while I call your mother."

In a cold, clipped voice, I overheard him telling my mother of the rape and my suicide attempt. "No, no police. She's okay, but I don't think she should be left alone." A long silence was followed by, "Okay, then, I'll have her there by nightfall. Good-bye now, Veronica." After hanging up the phone as if it weighed two hundred pounds, he looked off to the side and took some deep breaths. Then, with a blank expression on his face, he said, "Hurry up now and get your things."

Whimpering in desperation, I tried to explain, "But Joey, I had just met him at the shoe store. We started talking about dance contests. He said he was just going to get a sport coat so we could go dancing at another club after we danced at Whiskey-A-Go-Go's. He said he'd only be a minute and wanted me to see some fighter fish he had just purchased. He seemed really nice the whole evening. Besides, I knew where he works and lives, so how could he think I wouldn't tell the police? How could I have known he was dangerous?"

The muscles in his jaw were jumping up and down, indicating that his anger was escalating. He said, "Just shut up, Dawn! I'm driving you back home right now, so get your stuff together as fast as you can like I told you to do."

Familiar with his look—it was the one he'd get just before putting his fist into a wall—I shut my mouth and struggled to pack my few belongings. My head was pounding from the residual effects of booze, gas fumes, and Valium. I didn't have the will to argue.

I had only seen my mother once since we got married. When I tried to tell her of our troubles, she got up and walked out of our apartment without a word, so now I wondered what she would say, if anything, about a suicide attempt.

I didn't have the energy to fight my soon-to-be ex-husband and my mother, too, as they once again decided my fate. Besides, I knew that I would no longer feel safe alone in my apartment knowing that my rapist knew where I lived.

After gathering my few belongings and closing up my apartment, I followed Joey to the car. I knew I was justly liable for the drunken stupidity that had allowed me to ultimately bend to Joey's anger. I blamed myself, compounding my culpable position. Physically weak and emotionally defeated, I obeyed this demand to pack up and move back to my mother's house.

Joey's refusal to call the police was like a knife in my heart. I felt hurt and angry that my being brutally attacked would come second to maintaining the reputable status of his family name.

***

Our Volkswagen had never seemed as small as it felt now with the suffocating silence between us. Joey's face remained frozen in repressed fury for the entire trip as we drove to San Diego. I recalled this exact feeling in the car a year and a half earlier, when we drove to Los Angeles after our wedding. His silence on that day, just like today, had caused my insides to shrivel. I wondered why the isolation and silence felt so punishing to me. I knew that one word from me would unleash an explosion. Whether rigid silence blanketed the atmosphere with my mother or with Joey, that feeling of cold distance brought feelings of panic and abandon. I tried holding my breath in an attempt to reduce these emotions. I shrank into my seat.

Once again, as Joey dropped me off at the curb in front of my mother's house, I felt like a bundle of dirty laundry. I wanted to die when he left me standing there with only a dismissive wave of his hand. A cold feeling went through me, as if ice water were flowing through my veins. Alone once again, I watched his car fade out of sight.

Tears were flowing down my cheeks; I was sure I would never see him again. I would miss him intensely. I would miss his laugh, his humor, and his words—but not his anger. Oh, how I loved to string his words on that imaginary clothesline in my mind, hanging up one glorious phrase after another. His brilliance mesmerized me. It had been a long time since we had kissed, but the thought of never feeling his soft lips again, the kisses that once melted my knees, now broke my heart. My Joey was gone. How could everything in my life have gone so terribly wrong? Why couldn't I belong somewhere?

"Please God, why won't you just let me die? I hate you! I hate you!" Filled with anguish, so breathless I was gasping, I slowly picked up my suitcase and turned toward the house.

Heartsick, I thought about having come full circle just before entering the home I'd fought so hard to leave. I remember thinking as I opened the front door, "What happened to that feisty seventeen-yearold girl who oozed such gumption? The part of me that fought for values as if they mattered, as if *I* mattered?"

Where had she gone? Now I felt as blank as if I had merged with an old white sheet blowing aimlessly in the wind. Had it really been only eight hours since I sought permanent relief beneath the hissing gas stove? Had I broken yet another commandment, "Thou shall not kill?" *Who cares anyway?* I lamented. *I'm done with you, God! Do you hear me? I'm finished with you and your empty promises! Finished!*

I no longer wanted to please my beloved prince or even the king of kings. My promiscuity was meant to overcome my obsession with retribution, but in the end, I became what my mockers knew I was all along—soiled, tainted, and discarded, without any means of redemption. I doubted that my prince would ever know the murder of my soul that his words had imposed. I was on my own, alone, done.

***

Closing the front door took enormous effort; it felt like demons were pushing and pulling between me and the door. I met my mother's eyes as she looked up from the television. Weighing about two hundred pounds now that she rarely left the couch—and dressed in one of her brightly colored muumuus—she turned her Valium-coated eyes toward me. Her empty eyes rarely strayed from the television set, yet I thought I detected something resembling compassion, or maybe pity, because her eyes were looking at me in an uncharacteristically soft, almost loving, way.

Her words were softly simple, "Hi, how was the drive from Los Angeles?"

"Fine," I said with sudden exhaustion as I dropped my suitcase on the floor and sank down into the old plastic chair.

My grandmother, holding her Bible in one hand and her cigarette in the other, asked, "Where's Joey?"

Knowing how much they both loved Joey, and not wanting to hurt their feelings, I mumbled, "He had to get right back to Los Angeles."

"Oh!" they both said in unison. After what seemed like an eternity of familiar silence, I said wearily "I'm tired now. I'm going to lie down."

"Okay, dear," they said simultaneously. Briefly, the thought crossed my mind that my mother and grandmother had lived together for so long, they were now like Siamese twins in their thoughts and words.

Neither my mother nor my grandmother asked why I had wanted to die. At the time, I thought they lacked concern. Now I understand how they must have choked on their terror—especially my grandmother, for while she had never been physically affectionate, I was her main source of sunshine. In this family, there was no protocol for airing feelings. In fact, that was dangerous territory; it was best to just smile and forget. I realize now that it was not for lack of love or concern, it was just the proven means by which to *get through*. It was the *getting through life's trials* that both triumphed and trumped all other survival endeavors.

Without the knowledge of soothing words to offer me in that distress, my mother and grandmother instead allowed the comforting arms of sleep to wrap themselves around my weary body for three whole days. At various times during those days of darkness, I overheard them say to my younger brother, Russell, "Hush, your sister is resting." This seemingly tender reverence toward me did bring comfort. Allowing me to sleep was the most priceless gift Mother and Grandmother had to offer.

As if resurrected, I woke on the third day with new determination. Devising another plan of escape, I would fulfill a lifelong dream and become a stewardess, moving as far away as I could from those who knew my truth—the truth that seemed to be branded on my forehead. I may be soiled, I may be damaged goods, but, by God, I was determined.

Earning My Wings

LOOKING OUT OF the small airplane window, I felt a shiver run through my whole body as the plane climbed out over the San Diego Bay. I would miss my beloved beaches, but not the bad recollections that I assumed were forever associated with California. At age nineteen, I believed that distance erased, or at the very least diminished, bad memories.

Smooth as butter, the plane landed in Miami. Stepping out of the plane into the summer of 1965, I was assaulted with what I would come to understand as humidity. I thought that I was literally being strangled by the wet, muggy air. I kept looking all around me to see how other people were doing. I actually thought that something was terribly wrong. Everyone else seemed to be breathing just fine, which was somewhat reassuring. I quickly and gratefully headed to the hotel where I was being housed by the airlines pending a job interview in an airconditioned automobile. I sighed with relief as my head rested against the backseat. It had been a long day of travel from coast to coast.

My emotions alternately ran from excited anticipation to alarming dismay. Both feelings scared me. I closed my eyes as my thoughts unwillingly drifted over the last few months.

With newfound fervor, I had applied to every airline within the United States. I was turned down by most of them. They said I was considered "damaged merchandise" because I had been married. It seemed only young, skinny, untarnished girls were in demand. Thankfully, National Airlines flew me from San Diego to Miami for an interview. Following an exhausting, two-day interrogation—and despite my trepidation about an impending polygraph test (fearing it would somehow uncover my tainted core)—I was provisionally hired. Not considered a "real" stewardess until my divorce was finalized, I would remain on probation indefinitely.

Ever since age sixteen, when my beloved high school counselor gently informed me about my borderline retardation based on my I.Q. test results, I had felt as if I had a stamp on my forehead that read "DUMB"—but I all but flew through that airline cross-examination process, including the dreaded polygraph test, with flying colors.

Learning the airline language (like "Aft of the aft buffet"), the endless flight regulations, all major airport codes, how to operate emergency systems and safety equipment, water survival tactics, company rules, personal grooming and, of course, airline appearance standards, was all quite a challenge for me. Of the many girls at the beginning of our training, two did not make it to graduation. We were all housed together for the entire six weeks at a hotel in Miami. While the other girls slumbered peacefully, I studied by flashlight under the covers late into the night, so great was my fear of failure and my determination to change my life.

Completing the rigorous six-week stewardess training program left me feeling smashingly proud of myself. The day I graduated and received my wings, I knew I had made a giant step forward in my life. Finally, I had become *somebody*. Me! Imagine! And I had done it against all odds.

Acquiescent toward my new responsibilities—and, as was required, always smiling—I appeared to be doing well. Inwardly, I was reeling from relocating clear across the United States, my recent rape and attempted suicide, losing Joey, my uncontrolled drinking, and my bout with promiscuity. In spite of my lovely new job, there was a place deep inside me that was emotionally and spiritually exhausted, and my heart still ached for Joey. Every time I heard the song "I Wish You Love," I wept.

So many changes had happened within the past four months that I could hardly get oriented into a normal lifestyle. After flight training, I rented an apartment with three other stewardesses I had met during the training. Adjusting to three complete strangers was a mind-boggling experience. Miami itself was a culture shock to me. Adding to the mix was the steamy humidity. Every time I stepped out the front door, beads of sweat formed on my forehead. I felt suffocated by the density of the air, and my hair went limp.

Still on probation as a trainee, in addition to my provisional status as married, I was nevertheless allowed to fly. From the beginning, I loved every moment. It turned out that I was a *great* stewardess. Flying was still somewhat of a novelty for many people in the mid-sixties, and passengers were apprehensive about the whole experience. I loved caring for them and helping them to feel safe and comfortable. I truly adored waiting on people. I valued the opportunity to represent the airline that I now proudly worked for. I loved the adventurous feeling of take-offs and landings. I treasured the hustle and bustle of the airports, hotels, new people, and new places. I loved it all.

Most of all, I *loved* my uniform. Every time I stepped into that little black dress, adorned with my white hat and white gloves, I hugged myself with glee. The uniform proved that I had arrived—that I was indeed as good as anyone else. This new badge of honor bolstered my battered psyche. Another triumph was my beautiful silver wing pin, something I could actually hold in my hand and wear on my clothes as visible proof of my worthiness.

My only apprehensions were those concerning the pilots—who many of us revered like fathers, the ultimate authority figures (or even gods)—and the dreaded, mandatory weight checks. In order to meet the company's standards, our matching bubble hairdos, permitted shade of lipsticks, regulation Timex watches, and weigh-ins were all inspected by a supervisor prior to each flight.

Supervisor Stevens said, "Step on the scale, Dawn."

Shaking with fear, I stood on the large, hospital-like scale. "I was careful with my food this week, Mrs. Stevens."

"Not that careful—you still weigh 125 pounds, Miss DiMaggio." Through her lips, tight like a prune, she said, "Do you see this chart posted right here? It clearly states that at 5 feet 4 inches a woman should weigh 115 pounds. So, once again, I'll have to place you on probation." I held my breath as she began poking my sides, my arms, and my stomach. "Well, at least you're solid."

"I'm sorry, Mrs. Stevens, I really am trying."

Waving me through the door toward the plane, she said, "Trying will not cut it. Now, go!"

Those nerve-racking episodes reminded me of my old high school shower days. I hated the feeling that someone had power over my body. Breathing in a sigh of relief that I got through the unpleasant ordeal once again, I began thinking of lunch.

After a small breakfast earlier that morning, for the first time, I stuck my finger down my throat and threw up, hoping to weigh less. I had never seen or heard of anyone doing such a thing, but throwing up after eating occurred to me as the most logical way to pass my weight inspection. I wondered if my mother had been right all along, developing from a graceful racehorse to looking like a goddamn plow horse. Overcome with a sense of weariness as I headed for the plane, I forgot where it was that we were headed today. Not that it really mattered; I always felt lost.

Pulling my small suitcase behind me, I wondered if today's crew would be nice or indifferent. Some of the more experienced stewardesses seemed resentful at having to train us. I could understand that, since we trainees were often slow and clumsy. Just yesterday, when the plane hit an air pocket, I was not carrying the tray properly and I dumped twelve small plastic glasses of lemonade on a passenger's head while he was sleeping. Mortified, I scrambled to clean him off. The man goodd-naturedly said, "Don't worry, Honey; as long as it wasn't booze, I have no problem." Boy, would my old gym teacher have a field day seeing me now. I thought how perfectly her favorite nickname, Grace, fit me.

The pilots scared the daylights out of me because they held so much power over the flight attendants in those days. I was told that pilots could have you fired without any real cause if they became dissatisfied with your work. Ostensibly, their power to have a stewardess fired was strictly work-related, but we all knew that it could be something as petty as a pilot having his advances rejected. Perceiving potential danger, I tried to stay clear and not make any mistakes while tending to them during flights.

I also tried hard not to do or say stupid things, but sometimes the most unconscious questions would tumble out of my mouth. On my first trip to New York, I was riding in a van with the flight crew on our way to the hotel, bubbling over with excitement. I was beside myself see-ing the tall skyscrapers for the first time. I spied some horse-drawn carriages driven by men wearing top hats, tuxedos, and white gloves while navigating through traffic with their huge horses. I had never seen the likes of animals so grand, or men dressed so dashingly.

Excitedly, I asked, "Wow, are those real horses?"

Captain Dave looked at me with an expression somewhere between disgust and disbelief, and replied in a voice sopping with sarcasm, "No, Dawn, those are fake horses who eat synthetic oats."

I was so embarrassed I bit my lip to keep from crying. I knew right away that I had said yet another stupid thing. I was always saying stupid things or asking stupid questions. I had not yet learned how to bring forth questions in a logical, sequential manner. Words, thoughts, and questions ran around in my head at lightning speed. I merely blurted out the first vision that showed up on my thought-screen.

***

Painfully self-conscious about my mistakes, I often wondered how similar embarrassing moments of inappropriate blurting and mispronounced words affected Marilyn Monroe's presence in her world. I remember when, after I had said some ignorant thing or other, Joey said to me (in a rare, tender voice that was uncommon when he was giving me a reprimand), "God, you are so like Marilyn." When I asked him what he meant, he responded, "Oh, kind of dumb and kind of smart." Not wanting to know if this was a good thing or a bad thing, I let it drop.

In *After the Fall*, a thinly disguised portrayal of Marilyn, Arthur Miller repeatedly describes the dialogue of Maggie (Marilyn) speaking while using incorrect sentence structure. It was painful to see myself reflected in her inept, unaware, uneducated forms of communication. As grown women, when feeling scared, criticized, or demeaned, the realization and pressure of our inadequacies would exacerbate both Marilyn's and my stuttering problems.

How does one bear such self-incriminations? I will tell you how: alcohol! Alcohol made me feel pretty, competent, and smart. I wonder if it worked the same way for Marilyn. She certainly soared before her final crash-landing. For me, crash-landings came before soaring. Terrifying touchdowns and burning crash-landings were customary in my life before and during the coming years.

Stealing Booze and Crash-Landing

AFTER THREE MONTHS of adjusting to the climate as best as I could, mostly by staying in the air-conditioning, fall arrived, bringing welcome relief. I lived within a few miles of Miami International Airport, so cab fares were quite inexpensive. I loved the pastel colors of Coral Gables and the lushness of Coconut Grove. It seemed as if everywhere I went there was a body of water; the ocean, lakes, canals, and blue swimming pools were everywhere the eye could see. Some-times I even sighted a flock of beautifully multicolored wild parrots flying overhead. South Florida was truly a beautiful place to live.

Stealing had never been one of my early-life transgressions—except for twice when I was under the age of ten. While I dreaded the thought of being caught and losing my dream job, I began to sneak one or two miniature bottles of booze off the plane to soothe myself during our layovers. This violation was sure to get me fired if I were caught.

Since the rape, I just couldn't seem to get myself into any type of feeling of normalcy, (as if my behaviors prior to that time were "normal"). If a door closed loudly, or something dropped on the floor, I would jump as if a bomb had exploded or stand frozen on the spot.

On several occasions while flying, other stewardesses commented on my jumpy behavior. I tried to laugh it off, but felt even more nervous realizing they noticed. This left me constantly believing I was going to be found out. I didn't have a clue as to what it was that someone might find out about me, but that did not stop the internal alarm. Magnifying my discomfort were my recurring nightmares. In these dreams, people were laughing at me while I ran in tiny circles, trying to escape, but I could never find the door. Every day I told myself to just hang on, just hang on, just hang on. I had no idea, how long, or in what way—I just knew I should "Just hang on."

***

I knew nothing about grieving in those days; I just knew that my heart ached for Joey. My Joey, the boy I talked with for so many hours and thought about when he wasn't with me. I missed the tender kisses and the words that I used to hang, one by one, on the imaginary clothesline in my mind. They were treasured words, not unlike beautiful fragments of fine linen that I might want to pull out and save when I was alone. I wanted to feel, touch, even taste the deliciousness of each word. I sat at his feet, wide-eyed and adoring, perhaps the way Marilyn used to do with Arthur Miller.

I truly missed our far-too-brief friendship, and Joey's expressions of wisdom. I thought a lot about our failed marriage. Reminiscing as I often did in those days, I recalled the evening when I severely cut my right thumb and severed the tendons while washing dishes, which required an emergency room visit and many stitches. Within four weeks I had created another accident by lighting a match to a gas oven that someone had already turned on, which resulted in second and third-degree burns on my face and arms. Joey got so mad at me.

He hollered, "Stop hurting yourself, Dawn! You're subconsciously causing these things to happen to yourself."

Shocked at his words, I replied, "What are you talking about, Joey? All of these things were accidents. Why in the world would I do it on purpose?"

"I don't know why you keep hurting yourself, but you have no idea how powerful the mind is. We create our experiences by our unconscious beliefs."

His words gave me pause, adding to my idealized beliefs that he was brilliant and wise beyond his years. Oh, how I would miss him.

***

After a long three-day training flight, I was glad to be home. I closed the front door and looked at the calendar on the dining room table. I breathed a sigh of relief. Yes! I saw that my three roommates would be out of town for the next few days on training flights. Smiling to myself, I felt grateful for the much-needed time alone. I decided to celebrate with a hot bath and a can of chicken noodle soup that I had hidden from my roommates.

Weary from the training flight and difficulties with sleeping, I also planned on getting some deep rest. As I hung up my coat, anger coursed through me: one of my roommates had taken my other uniform. We were each issued one uniform upon completion of flight training and had to purchase a second one, which was quite expensive. My mother had scraped together the money for my extra uniform. Trainees were perpetually on standby, so we never knew when we would be called out on a flight. A clean backup uniform was imperative. Irritated that I now had to take my dirty uniform to the dry cleaners on my one day off, I wondered how my roommate could be so rude and selfish.

While thinking how I could wring her cute little neck, I jumped, bumping my head on a wooden shelf, at the sound of the doorbell.

Looking through the front door peephole, I was shocked to my core. It was Joey!

He had driven our little VW wagon across the United States from Los Angeles to Miami, and announced that he had come to "take me back." After his three-thousand-mile journey, he looked as exhausted as I felt. I was elated to see him, and we fell into each other's arms.

We spent a delightful afternoon and early evening walking and talking with the same kind of ease and wonderment we experienced the first week we'd met two years earlier.

"How are your parents, Joey?"

"Oh, you know, everything is kind of the same. I haven't talked with my dad since way before you left California. And Dorothy, well, not much communication there either. She and Bob have sure been drinking a lot lately. They're uncomfortable to be around."

"Jeez, Joey, it sounds kind of lonely for you."

Joey, changing the mood, picked me up by the waist and swung me around. I loved the feel of his hard, muscular body close to me. I could tell he had been working out again because his white sport shirt barely fit around the muscles in his arms. "Yeah, Babe. That's why I need you back in my life. I need my buddy."

At that, we both laughed now with that hollow kind of laugh you do when you know you've just skipped right over a river of painful feelings.

I loved his brown eyes and strong jawline (when it was relaxed, as opposed to the too many times when he was angry or just not communicating). Stroking the tiny, fine, golden-brown hairs on his arm, I couldn't let go of him. Over pizza at a little Italian restaurant, he told me some hilarious stories about his adventures during the past few months, and kept injecting into his narrative the words of how much he had missed me. That day we were stuck together like glue. We kissed, ate, talked, kissed, laughed, walked, and kissed. So happy to be with him again, I never once considered where this encounter was leading, or how it would inevitably end.

Long after sundown, we drove to the beach and were caught by the Miami Beach police while snuggled in the comforting, warm sand and necking. After convincing them that we were indeed married, as proven by our matching driver's license names, they merely scolded us before telling us to leave the beach at once. Giggling at each other, we drove back to my place, blissfully unprepared for the ugly last scene that was about to unfold—the final chapter of our lives together.

Back inside of the apartment, I started getting nervous. Sure enough, Joey pulled me into the bedroom, pulling off my shirt and simultaneously undressing himself.

My stomach began to churn with fear as my mind began showering me with past film clips of our bedroom history. I walked out of the bedroom.

"No, Joey, let's not start this. Okay?" "Don't be silly, you're still my wife."

"No, Joey, I'm not coming back to the bedroom."

"God damn it, Dawn, quit acting stupid and get back in here now!" "Noooooo! I'm not coming in there!"

Angry, with hands on his hips in a defiant posture he said, "Listen, Dawn, if you don't stop this crap right now, when I get back to California I'll tell the authorities that we lived together during our interlocutory period and our divorce process will be nullified immediately. Then what'll you do, Miss High-and-Mighty?"

I muttered something unintelligible; but then, instead of my usual, shame-filled, compliant, little-girl attitude, an ire began bubbling in me, like the pressure building in a geyser soon to erupt.

He threatened, "D-o y-o-u understand me?"

With equal anger I shouted, "If you do that, Joey, I'll tell the newspapers the truth about our sex life. I swear, Joey, I'll tell it all."

"You wouldn't do that, Dawn. You didn't tell that magazine anything even after they offered you all that money to talk about your impressions of *the great "Joltin' Joe."* Come on, you know you're way above that sort of thing."

"You stop threatening me, Joey, or I swear I'll tell!"

"God damn you! I trusted you. What's happened to you these past few months anyway? You're not the Dawn that I knew. In fact, you're acting just like all the rest of the people in my life."

"Joey, I want you to leave now. Please, I beg of you, just go."

We argued, cried, and then argued again. It was ugly and painful for both of us, but I could not bring myself to repeat the cycle of tenderness, passion, and failed orgasms, only to be followed by harsh and demeaning accusations. Becoming a stewardess had given me new strength and more than a little of some much-needed self-esteem.

I begged him over and over to leave. Finally, spent from anger and grief, we stood at the doorway, sobbing in each other's arms, knowing full well that we would never see each another again. I was engulfed in an anguish so deep that I fell to my knees, sobbing, "Joey, Joey," as he walked out the door. I lay in an inconsolable heap until I remembered the bottle of vodka under the kitchen sink that belonged to the room-mate who had taken my clean uniform. She owed me.

***

Within hours of Joey's departure, I was drunk. All I cared about was escaping the pain. Running away always seemed to be a solution, like when I was a little girl and ran to the arms of the eucalyptus trees. I threw clothes into a suitcase and got a cab to the bus station, where I boarded a Greyhound for New York City. Why New York? Who knows?

Two days later, disheveled, hungry, and with little money, I checked into a sleazy hotel in New York City. In sheer panic, I called my super-visor and quit my beloved job, pretending a lengthy family emergency.

Just prior to my entering the six-week stewardess training program, I had begun dating a handsome man sixteen years my senior. We were introduced by a mutual friend. Bill held a Bachelor of Science degree and was a showroom manager at the Miami Playboy Club. Suave and debonair, he began pressuring me to marry him within weeks of our ini-tial meeting. Although he was thirty-six, he had never married. I took his interest in me to be true love. I did not return his attention with a feeling of "love," but I was interested in his seeming maturity, self-assurance, and sincerity. I had half-heartedly considered his offer, pon-dering if after my first marital experience I would ever feel comfortable with a man of worldly experience.

Considering the lack of viable options, I called Bill and agreed to marry him. After explaining the whole incident about Joey's visit, get-ting drunk, and fleeing to New York, he seemed quite amused, even glib. He immediately planned to fly to New York—where he was orig-inally from—and gather me up to save me from myself and my penni-less predicament.

Bill said, "Don't worry about a thing, Honey, being a stewardess is nothing more than being a waitress without the tips. I'm glad you got out of all that nonsense. Now we can settle down and get started on making a family. I'll fly up tomorrow and you can meet my family. As soon as we get back to Miami next week, we'll get married. I'll take care of everything, you just relax and I'll see you tomorrow."

Hanging up the phone, I asked myself why I didn't feel relieved. If anything, I felt a million times worse. *Oh God, oh God, what have I done?* It was clear that I wasn't capable of taking care of myself, which caused a feeling of self-hatred so deep within me that I felt as if my insides had just been branded with a hot poker. Now I would have another new boss. I knew he would rule my life, but I felt that I deserved this fate. I buried my throbbing head into my pillow and sobbed myself to sleep.

Bill flew to New York and rescued me, just like the scenario that had played itself out weeks prior to my marriage to Joey. Then, it was Joey who came to Los Angeles; this time, it was Bill who came to New York. On neither of these occasions did I want to get married, but, driven by shame and alcohol-influenced decisions, I succumbed. I didn't know it then, but this time, my decision to have Bill rescue me in the form of marriage was like choosing to die by fire versus dying by hanging.

My decision was born out of a defeated form of survival. The *barely hanging on* form of survival. I could never have imagined the peril and the terror that that single decision would put into effect for decades to come. Even my snarled, drunken insides screamed at me not to choose another marriage as a solution to my current crisis, but by then I was beyond defeated, which only left grasping.

Without a single internal resource left to draw upon, I sold my soul for the illusion of safety. Just as I had done so long ago as a hungry child by allowing touching in exchange for candy, I bartered for a piece of sustenance and paid the price in desolation.

***

Years later, I would learn how Joey handled his grief later that night after we said good-bye. He stumbled (accidentally?) onto a houseboat in Miami where Larry King was broadcasting a nighttime radio show, and he spilled his guts to King. The following interview was mentioned in Larry King's memoir, then reprinted in Richard Ben Cramer's *Joe DiMaggio: The Hero's Life.*

Joe Jr.: "I never knew my father. My parents were divorced when I was little and I was sent away to a private school. My father was totally missing from my childhood. When they needed a picture of father and son, I'd get picked up in a limo and have my picture taken. We were on the cover of the first issue of *Sport* magazine when it came out in 1949, my father and me. I was wearing a little number 5 jersey. I was driven to the photo session, we had the picture taken, and I was driven back. My father and I didn't say two words.

"I cursed the name I had, Joe DiMaggio Jr. While at Yale I played football—I deliberately avoided baseball—but when I ran out on the field and they announced my name, you could hear the crowd murmur. When I decided to leave college and join the Marines, I called my father to tell him. You know, you call your father when you make lifechanging decisions like that. When I told him, he said, 'The Marines are a good thing.' And that was it. There was nothing more for either of us to say."

"DiMaggio, Jr. said the closest he'd ever been to his father was in the car on the way to Marilyn Monroe's funeral in 1962. He said his father had always gone on loving Monroe and that he loved her, too . . ."

It has been widely reported that Joey D. did not see his father in the last years of Joe Sr.'s life, and was left the relatively small sum of $20,000 in the will.

Joey finished his life living alone in a junkyard trailer in northern California. Within six months of his father's death, Joey, at fifty-seven, was dead from years of drug and alcohol abuse.

Marie

NINETEEN AND TWICE-MARRIED, I had become a woman lost. There was no me to be found anywhere inside. Like an obedient puppy, I did what I was told to do. Whipped by life, I had become unable to make even the simplest decision on my own. For example, if I was driving and came to a stop sign, and wasn't sure which way to turn, I would cover my face and sob while my car sat in the middle of the intersection. All of my previous coping mechanisms had failed me. Hope had failed me. I had failed me.

For six long years, I remained in this impotent state, blindly abiding by my husband's every word. Then, a single incident pushed me into a direction of pure defiance. Just like the rebellious part of me that started a field fire at age seven or the self-hatred-and-rage-filled sexual acting out.

The following story is an example of how passive-aggressive my behaviors could be. It also became a profound defining moment for me.

The car horn honked lightly in my driveway. My neighbor, Carol, was taking me Christmas shopping. I could think of nothing else all day for weeks since I had planned this day. Rarely permitted to leave the house, I was filled with excitement. The house was immaculate; my three babies were spic and span and quietly tucked away in their beds for the night. Pot roast and potato smells wafted through the house while my husband's dinner warmed in the oven. I had made him an extra-special meal in exchange for allowing me to go out for the evening. Of course, he was late coming home this particular evening. Already nervously anticipating a problem, I explained to him that all he had to do was pull his dinner from the oven. I had to run hearing Carol's horn honk louder this time.

I grabbed my purse saying "Ok, gotta run now." Out of the corner of my eye I thought I noticed an intimidating expression beginning to change the contour of his face. I held my breath, too afraid to look, hoping to escape before his deluge of angry accusations and/or criticisms poured forth from his mouth.

"Dawn, there are some toys under the playpen." *Oh God*, I thought, *not now, please just this once, not now.* "I will pick them up when I get home, Carol is waiting." Having been through enough of these scenes with my husband of six years, my stomach began to hurt, and my shoulders were up to my ears with apprehension. "You will pick up those toys now or you won't go," he said.

All of a sudden, I was overcome with a feeling of such determination that I did not recognize myself. I walked to the couch, sat down, and, folding my arms, I looked him directly in the eye. He said, "Look at you, sitting there acting like a two-year-old instead of doing what you are supposed to do." I got up and waved Carol on without me. She knew enough of the situation to have guessed what had just happened. I sat back on the couch, waiting for his torrent of controlled, strategic insults.

For the first time since I had married this man, I was dauntless. It's not that I wasn't afraid—he had hit me before—but by God, this time I was going down fighting. It was as if a dam of potency broke within me, filling every fiber of my being with bravery. I remember thinking, *Go ahead and break my arms if you must, but I will not pick up those toys.* After what seemed like an eternity, I stood up and walked to the door. He slowly walked toward me, dramatically taking my purse and pulling out the thirty dollars of Christmas money and my house keys.

"Now, if you walk out that door, you will never see your kids again." I kept walking. I walked a few miles to a bar and got drunk. I rarely drank since marrying Bill. Four days later, I filed for divorce. Free again to drink without accountability, I drank as often as I could, even lacing my milk with scotch to soothe my gut-wrenching ulcer.

That night I eventually made my way to my friend Marie's house to spend the night. Her husband called to tell my husband that I was okay and there for the night since it was three o'clock in the morning by the time they arrived home from a party. My husband said, "Kick her out, do not let her stay there." Guy begged my husband to be reasonable, but he insisted that I be thrown out. I stayed for the weekend. Guy was never forgiven for his betrayal.

Marie wanted me to go back with my husband for the sake of the children. She knew that I had no way to support myself and the children, and was only capable of getting a minimum-wage job. She also told me that she would stand by me in whatever choice I made. On Monday I went before a judge, who ordered me back into the house and my husband out. Thus began my odyssey to become self-supporting. I am grateful to Marie, who was my champion then and during the previous two years.

***

When I see old reviews of the humorous and touching 1988 movie *Cocoon: The Return*, I can't help but think of my friend Marie. She was a professional makeup artist for television and motion pictures. In the late sixties I even got to watch her work when she invited me to lunch on the set of the then-popular television series *Gentle Ben*.

To most of the world Marie is an unknown, but not to many people whose very career hinged on her talents. She was responsible for helping some very famous people put on their best face for the public. She encouraged them to "Get out there and knock 'em dead!" almost every time she made contact with them. She was a "hands-on" person that was completely intimate with every little blemish or flaw, inner and outer, that the celebrities she worked with had. She often worked, long hours to bring out the inner charm and beauty of each one. And so, in the end, her work will remain visible for generations to see and, hopefully, admire.

I had met her at a luncheon for ex-stewardesses. For some mysterious reason, we bonded immediately. Then, our husbands, armored with their collective Italian heritages and involvement with the movie industry, become fast friends.

We were the most unlikely candidates for a lifelong friendship. I was twenty-three and she was thirty-three. Feeling ashamed of my ignorance, I rarely looked anyone in the eye. I thought they might see my ignorance as if ignorance itself was branded around the edges of my cornea. Marie was different; with her, I could share my deepest thoughts uncensored. We enthusiastically discussed marriage, societies, world religions, and philosophy. It was not as if I really knew anything about these subjects, but I came alive with the opportunity to even be discussing such things. Spellbound by her extensive knowledge, I was stunned that she found my opinions interesting.

Really, we were an improbable match for any type of relationship. I was a young wife—shy, frightened, and uneducated, with three small children. She was beautiful, worldly, fluent in three languages, well-educated, and a nationally known makeup artist who had chosen not to have children. I could barely put together any type of clear, cogent sentence. For reasons that will forever remain a mystery to me, she saw a seed of value in me. She believed in me.

I remember the day she brought lunch to my home and we talked as my three babies napped. She was so excited about a night course in psychology, I think it was called "The Self," that was being offered at the local community college. She wanted me to take it with her.

At first, I thought she must be crazy. I shamefacedly told her the results of my high school IQ test, still convinced of my "borderline retarded" prognosis. I told her about being placed in remedial classes. I did not comprehend grammar, spelling, or parts of speech, and told her to *please* not even talk to me about numbers. Seemingly simple tasks with numbers often appeared backwards in my mind. Likewise, I could rarely fit those funny-shaped little pieces of wood, used in intelligence tests, into their rightful slots. "No, Marie, I could not possibly take this course with you."

Like throwing a rope to a slowly drowning person, she persisted. I had been lost in a sea of despair and endless struggle for *my entire life*. All through our friendship, her interest in me, her belief in me, and her trust was something I had never experienced before. She stirred something deep within me because she responded to me as if my opinion held a modicum of intelligence, as if I had value. I think the *something* she saw in me was a profound hunger. A burning appetite I didn't even know I had, and an enthusiasm for knowledge that I was convinced it wasn't possible for me to attain. Had I met her sooner, I might not have believed those who proclaimed that I was dumb or a "little" retarded.

She begged me to take this college-level psychology course with her. She said that *she* needed the support. I eventually went because I loved her and wanted to repay her many kindnesses to me. My husband, Bill, said that I would make a fool of myself and show my stupidity for the entire world to see.

I received an "A" in the course. Even after achieving my silver wings, I had never been so proud of any accomplishment in my life. A bona fide idiot according to the experts, I got an "A" in a college course, can you imagine? I so much wanted to hang that grade around my former husband's neck (and fit it very tight). By the time I received that grade in the mail, some three months after starting the course, I had left my marriage. Because Marie held up the unwavering possibility of success for me to step up to, she single-handedly breathed life into my weary being. For the next thirty years, I never stopped studying or taking one course or another.

I still can't spell very well, nor do I thoroughly understand parts of speech. Wooden squares, rectangles, and circles continue to con-found me, and numbers in any fashion are forgotten in a nanosecond. *And yet, I am smart*. In fact, I think it must take a special kind of intelligence to achieve what I have, academically, given the confines of my apparently malfunctioning brain. The psychologist who last tested me said I was "absolutely brilliant" in the area of common sense. She said the gap between my "common-sense knowledge" and my "academic knowledge" was the largest discrepancy she had ever seen.

Learning to believe in myself taught me that tenacity trumps shortcomings. Tenacity even trumps major learning disabilities. I suppose there is no way of testing desire, willingness, and perseverance, but if there were, I can imagine that a whole new world of possibilities and options would open up for thousands of people. Unfortunately, the IQ test remains the gold standard by which most everyone's intelligence is still measured.

Some forty years have passed since Marie lovingly coerced me into taking that class. I have since earned two master's degrees from major universities. My ending grade point average from both schools was just under 3.8. Many times, I had to withdraw from a course just before I crossed the point of failing, and then would immediately re-take the course. I always "got it" the second time around. I have held the position of adjunct professor. I have a successful counseling practice. I am proud of myself.

Marie has watched me grow over the years, and has thanked me for giving her life meaning; she once told me that I am her greatest success. Can you imagine? It is I who should thank her—I will be eternally grateful to her for setting me on the path to a new life.

But I am getting ahead of myself. Before I got to where I am today, I had several more hard lessons to learn.

Ruled by a hundred forms of shame, guilt, need, emptiness, hate, anxiety, false pride, and a makeshift persona, I was without balance or perspective, nothing more than a frenzied reactor greedily ripping and tearing through life.

> "We spend our life until we're twenty deciding what parts of ourselves to put in the bag, and we spend the rest of our lives trying to get them out again."
>
> —Robert Bly

There was little difference between me and the bag.

Seven Times Seven

IN DECEMBER OF 1972, my daughter had just turned five, and her twin brothers were four. The long and embittered divorce proceedings were finally ending for Bill and me. My now ex-husband contested my half-interest in all our assets, stating that I had not worked outside the home and therefore deserved nothing. The role of mother or housewife didn't represent anything of value in his mind. He was enraged by the eventual fifty/fifty financial split. A few days after the divorce was granted, he came to my apartment brandishing a gun. He pointed the gun right at my head and said, "I'll be keeping my eye on you, and you best understand that I have absolutely no qualms about using this." I was too fearful to tell the police or anyone else—not the first time I buckled to the pressure of a threat or harm.

The day after his threat he promptly departed for sunny California for an eight-month period to live with his friends Christopher and Lynda Day George.

Lynda and I met when we were nineteen. Our husbands went to college together, and had worked together on several "want-to-be" films. Whether it was our innate shyness, our lack of self-esteem, or our then-narcissistic partners, we bonded immediately. Perhaps it was our yet-undisclosed backgrounds of poverty and abuse that created a kind of familiarity that fostered our attachment. We had both had multiple fathers, alcoholism, abuse, knock-down drag-out family fights, little money or food, and pressure from our mothers for financial support while we were still in high school. Some would call our growing-up lifestyle hard times; others would call it trailer-trash.

Both of our mothers wanted us to support them financially. I escaped this mantle by marrying at age seventeen, thereby trading the temporary hell of financial extortion for the more permanent hell of matrimony. Lynda, on the other hand, succumbed to her family's desperation and became a teenage New York model. At five feet nine, gentle as a kitten, beautiful, and with perfect posture, she was helpless against the modeling agencies that sought her and the guilt heaped upon her to sustain a family living in poverty.

Lynda went on to become famous in her field, and yet to me, nothing of her sweet nature has changed since our first meeting. Lynda Day George became "known" when she appeared in the popular TV series

Mission Impossible (1970-1973) as Lisa Casey, a role for which she received a Golden Globe nomination.

One day while I was staying with Lynda, she took me to the set of *Mission Impossible*. It was fun meeting the cast and watching her work; but what will forever stand out in my mind and heart was what happened when we returned home. Lynda was wearing a light blue, pleated silk suit that looked beautiful on her. I told her how pretty she looked. That night, when I went to my room, there across the bed lay the suit with a note attached. The note said simply, "Enjoy, honey." I protested, but she insisted that I keep the suit. At only five feet four, I had to roll up the skirt at the waist, but I felt like a million bucks in that suit, and I wore it with pride for the next twelve years.

The best part of her gift was that I knew that she did not give it to me out of pity, even though Lynda knew that I was married to an extremely controlling man who prohibited me from buying clothes (or anything else, for that matter). I knew in my heart that Lynda gave me the suit out of generosity. That is just how Lynda was then and is now. We have remained close friends. But in the early seventies, living on different coasts and both struggling with difficult issues, we were unable to lend much support to each other.

***

After Bill and I divorced I worked for minimum wage as a receptionist in a security office located in a dangerous, run-down part of Miami. It was completely without possibility of advancement—first because it was a very small company without opportunities, and second, because I didn't deserve to advance. The company tolerated the myriad of mistakes I made on proposals, mainly because they were kind people. Fortunately, they liked me and felt sorry for my situation.

Having to take so much time off from work to attend to my son Ty's medical appointments forced me to quit this job. I was terrified without one, and my options were running out.

Ty also became the motivation for my budding assertiveness. I fought boldly for what I thought were his best interests. The doctors wanted to medicate my son to lessen his "acting out" behaviors, and to splint his arms so that he could not take the adhesive tape off of his good eye (to keep it from crossing); or they wanted him to continue in speech therapy, while I argued that he needed hearing aids. This initial solo crusade was a nightmare, since the medical professionals would not consider *my* observations regarding my son's hearing defects. When, some six years later, he was fitted with hearing aids, deafness proved to be one of his major problems. He also struggled with many problems stemming from his three-month premature birth. At age three, they wanted to put him on Ritalin. I declined. The doctors were exasperated at my supposed lack of cooperation.

While finding it difficult to stand up for myself prior to dealing with these doctors, I was bold and fierce when it came to defending the needs of my little boy. In doing so, without realizing it, I began constructing the basic building blocks of a substantial me.

Instead of the usual person's lunch bag tote, I carried a barf bag to accommodate my worsening ulcer. Compounding my physical sickness was acute anxiety and excessive exhaustion. My overall prevailing mental state was grim. But, by God, my son never missed *one day* of his special needs class, and I never missed *one day* of the real estate classes I was taking to become a licensed real estate salesperson. No matter how much my stomach hurt or how many times I had to excuse myself to use the bathroom, I was always present.

Circumstances were becoming desperate as Ty's need for medical treatment increased. When I arranged a carpooling situation with other mothers with special needs children, my son was suddenly prohibited from using the carpool due to his animalistic biting behavior. He would repeatedly tear off all of his clothes and physically attack the other children, primarily with his teeth. Now Ty, expelled from all day care centers, and eventually rejected by every available babysitter, presented a constant string of crises for me. Solutions seemed insurmountable without the assistance of an extended family or some exorbitant amount of money. His father refused to help out in any way, hoping that I would give up and return home where he thought I belonged. That, and he wanted revenge.

***

I met Bo in a sleazy bar four weeks after separating from Bill. Bo was charming and funny and had beautiful blue eyes and boyish good looks. He would become both my inspiration and my abuser.

Bo entered my life filled with hopeful possibilities for me. He suggested that I obtain a real estate license, which would place me in a job situation with flexible hours. I pointed out that I couldn't do that since I didn't even know my times tables. He offered to teach me. True to his word, we practiced reciting the times tables every night while I attended real estate school by day. Unfortunately, this knowledge did little to help me with the closing statement part of the real estate exam, but I was good at the law portion, so I concentrated my efforts there.

Though hired by a prestigious real estate office, I had no time to feel proud of myself: it was 1972, and the bottom had dropped out of real estate in southern Florida. So while I was learning the field, running down leads and pounding signs in overgrown front lawns, I simultaneously studied for my life and health insurance license.

I was driven by every form of imaginable fear. What if I ran out of money and I was unable to support myself or my children? What if I had no credit? What if I lost my children due to lack of money or some emotional or physical illness? The day would come when all of those fears would come to pass.

I spent half of the proceeds from my divorce buying a small two-bedroom house. I had also used part of the money to support the children and myself while I was getting started in real estate. I was mindful every waking moment that if I did not bring in money soon, I would run out of the divorce proceeds. Then, out of stupidity, I lent Bo four thousand dollars to open a gas station/convenience store. Not once did it occur to me that he would refuse to pay me back.

The fear and degradation of having to regress back to receiving welfare seemed more than I could endure. Moreover, I feared that if I did accept welfare, I would lose my house. Somehow, I had it in my mind that my children and I could withstand anything so long as we had a house, a safe haven to which we could return. I was desperate to save the small amount of possessions I had acquired. In my thinking, this thin veil of protection buffered my children and me against a perilous world. I believed that only I could protect them. And nobody, but nobody, understood Ty as I did.

When I was first divorced, according to the credit card companies, I was not permitted to obtain a credit card without my ex-husband's cosignature. *Over my dead body*, I thought. I marched over to Sears and applied for a three month revolving charge account. I have had perfect credit ever since. Single-minded of purpose, I was desperate and determined to never again rely on a man for my financial well-being. I would do whatever it took to make myself over and to make myself marketable in a financial capacity. I *had* to earn money, I *had* to be self-supporting.

***

Bo, who began our relationship with supportive ideas and encouragement, was fast becoming another tormentor. First, he became angry that my ex-husband had been living the high life in California instead of helping support our children. Bill had not worked in a year and had no involvement with his children, except for mailing his three-hundred-dollar child support check each month. Bo began pressuring me to let my children live with their father, who was now back in southern Florida. Bo knew that Bill's family had the money to help with the children's special needs. We fought extensively over this difficult situation, but I could not imagine life without my children. I also began to notice his possessiveness and the beginning of totally unfounded, jealous accusations.

One year into the relationship, signs of physical abuse began to emerge, though I did not recognize the warning signs. For example, he started badgering me about the number of men that I had *ever* slept with. With teeth clenched, and in that slow, deliberate, menacing voice some people get just before exploding, he would forcefully poke me in the arm or leg or back, while saying "And—poke—just— poke—how— poke—many—poke—men—poke—have—poke—there—poke— been? Huh—huh? How—poke—many?" I would refuse to answer.

***

My daughter, Alex, and Ty's twin brother, Jess, had age-appropriate sicknesses and little childhood traumas that needed tending, but Ty's hearing, eyesight, lack of speech, and overall delayed developmental issues were so huge that they became all-consuming. Every day, I struggled with bills, scheduling demands, sick children, and now a controlling boyfriend who wanted attention and sex. Just like when I was married, these stressors caused severe physical reactions. At least once a week, I had either an ulcer attack or spasmodic gastritis so painful that I spent all night on the bathroom floor.

Fast losing ground in a number of ways, the final straw came the day my health insurance premiums doubled. The premiums shot up to $350.00 monthly, which was more than my monthly child support checks. I was scared to death. My son's problems demanded that I maintain health insurance. My stress became apparent to everyone around me. I was losing weight, not sleeping, and stuttering more frequently, and my drinking and smoking increased.

Desperate, I rented out my little house and moved in with a girlfriend and her two young children. We worked together in the real estate office. We thought we could help each other with babysitting and expenses. Unbeknownst to me, she was already a full-blown alcoholic; and as circumstances proceeded, I was not far behind.

Then came the day I returned home and Ty had destroyed his bedroom. The curtains torn and shredded, the dresser drawers pulled out and overturned, the children's bedroom looked like it had been struck by a tornado. I hit Ty so hard across the face that I left a handprint on his cheek that lasted for the next few days. The look of stunned disbelief on my little boy's face will haunt me for the rest of my life. Shocked and devastated by my behavior, I felt all of my demons closing in. Nothing I tried dug us out of the black hole that was enveloping us. I had never hit my children before, and I did not want to become an abusive mother. It seemed I could no longer trust myself. I was defeated. In my insanity, I thought that God was punishing me for all of my past, sinful ways. Why else would He want to take away my babies?

Bo helped me devise a plan as a possible way to ease my situation. Since Bill had returned to Florida from California, there might be a way to force his assistance, even though he had refused to help with his son's transportation or in any matter regarding his children. The three of us decided that my roommate would drop the children off on their father's doorstep and say that I had gone to California in some measure of defeat. While I had become numb, Bo was elated to get rid of my children.

Once I knew the children were physically safe with their father, I did fly to California to see if my family could help with the children's care. I researched the possibility of any specialized aid, housing, and childcare for disabled children. I called my brother in Colorado and begged him to take my daughter and other son while working out a solution for myself and Ty's special needs. He was unable to do so. Nothing worked out. I was foiled. Defeated. Finished.

When I returned to Florida a few weeks later, I realized my earlier lie to my ex-husband was a mistake. Bill was now telling everyone, our children included, that I had abandoned them and that I had never loved or wanted them.

With my children now gone, my house rented, and my soul nowhere to be found, I moved in with Bo. It would be only a matter of time before the first beating occurred. Wounded targets are easy prey.

***

I don't remember much about the first beating except wondering what I had done to cause it. I determined that whatever it was I did, I would never do it again. Of course, he was very sorry and pointed out how I had brought it all upon myself. Just like in Catholic school, when he said I deserved the whacks, I believed him.

Bo also reminded me of my sexual inadequacies, patiently explaining that all of his other women were multi-orgasmic and that my single orgasm was quite disappointing. He fancied himself a great lover, when in truth he confused staying power with sensual expertise. He would not even kiss, much less caress. But at that time, those were not my thoughts. Inundated with past memories, I was sure that he was correct in his sexual assessment.

I believed from past experience with my first husband that I was truly a sexual disappointment. Ignorance, two failed marriages, three children, lack of money, sexual inadequacy, bleached-blond hair, and weekly vomiting did little to enhance my self-esteem. And now, adding to my list of self-incrimination, I was an abusive, abandoning mother, who was fast becoming a lush.

The second beating was totally unanticipated and unprovoked. I had just arrived home from work, and simply walked into the bathroom to wash my hands. The next thing I knew, he had me up against a wall pounding on my head and face. I was screaming and begging him to stop, all the while hearing a ringing in my ears. I did what I always do in the face of terror—I did nothing to escalate the situation. I stood frozen until I was spoken to, and with his permission I sat on a chair in the living room, waiting for him to make the next move. When he said I could leave, I carefully, and as quickly as possible, gathered as many belongings as I could carry to my car. With heart racing and tears streaming, I quietly drove off into the alone.

For the next week, I slept in my car, washing up in the early morning at my real estate office before anyone showed up for work. Unable to go to my rented house, I found an affordable apartment that didn't require the first and last month's rent. It was so dilapidated that the first time my daughter, Alex, now six, set eyes on it, she cried. I felt like the trailer trash that I thought I had long ago escaped being.

Eventually able to move back into my house, I now had to drive by the gas station that I had financed in order to get home. It took every ounce of restraint I could muster to not drive my car right through his/my plate glass window. The window I had unwittingly purchased in good faith now sparkled every day like a beacon, taunting my stupidity.

Over the next year I tried in vain to get the money that Bo owed me. My escalating rage over his theft frightened me. The last time I had felt that kind of rage I was seven years old and had set a field on fire. Fortunately for both of us, I feared his stalking behaviors more than I relished revenge and decided to leave well enough alone. As God is my witness, I could have killed him.

Ultimately, this was another turning point for me. It seemed necessary that I go through such extremes to learn some of life's most basic lessons. I would never again be anyone's physical or psychological punching bag. It became my bottom line deal-breaker in subsequent relationships.

Barefoot Under the Table

"DON'T EVER CALL me again!" my paternal grandmother warned harshly as she hung up the phone. This abrupt conversation, actually just an answer to my greeting of "Hello," left me bewildered. She and I had been having long-distance phone conversations for at least fifteen years. Sure, the conversations were brief, stiff, and unwelcome on her part, but many years ago, we had made a deal: if she would talk with me occasionally by phone, then I would not pursue the search for my father. I had kept my end of the bargain, so what in the world was the matter with her? I immediately called her back.

"Althea, what do you mean, what happened?"

This time she was angrier: "For God's sake, use your head!" She slammed down the phone again.

Recently divorced from Bill, living alone with three small children, no family nearby to help, and with little money, a minimum wage job, ulcers, and way too much booze, her rejection came at the worst possible time. Panic set in. I made myself a stiff drink, took a few sips of the liquid courage, and called her back for a third time. Pleading, I said, "Althea, you need to tell me what you're talking about."

Her reply this time was, "After all of these years wasting my time talking to you, I've spoken to my son. He assured me that you're positively not his child. Now leave me alone, and don't ever call this number again!"

The silence on the phone line was deafening—a different kind of silence than just a broken phone connection. This kind of silence was intended to eradicate all of the connecting bits and pieces that held people tenuously together. Her intention was to erase our pasts and any thoughts that I may be entertaining about meeting my father, her son. This sudden realization was overwhelming. I could hardly breathe. Oh God, I thought, not another loss!

My defiant response was, "Okay, then, but I will move forward with meeting my father."

She responded, "You gave your word that you'd never contact him."

"That was before you negated our contract!" Angry and heartbroken, I slammed down the phone and made another drink.

Even though her voice was cold and robotic all these years during our phone calls, she had been a connection to something positive about my beginnings. Sometimes I felt like a wild bird that migrates to some unfamiliar place, but a force within them tells them it's the right thing to do—a *needed* thing to do for survival.

I can only imagine the heartbreaking disappointment that Marilyn felt the day that she finally got up the nerve to call her father. Her first husband, Jim Dougherty, said that she slumped down, put the receiver back and said, "Oh, Honey, he hung up on me."

***

I had met my grandparents one time, briefly, when I was nineteen. Bill and I had driven up to New England to see his parents, and I persuaded him to make a side trip to "the grandparents'." While my grandmother was cold and aloof, my grandfather was warm and kind. The first words out of his mouth to me were, "You have eyes just like your father's." I would hang onto to those words for years to come because that matched exactly what my mother had said years prior. I would close my eyes and think about what the rest of my real father's face looked like. Did it look like mine? Did he have my hair color? Was his nose like mine?

For the next year, I planned the meeting with my father. Although I had an overpowering desire for connection and hopefully some validation, I forced myself to go slowly and devise a plan. I had learned over the years from this grandmother, albeit grudgingly, that he had a wife and five children. I did not want to harm this man or his family in any way. I only wanted a few moments of his time, a glance at his face, perhaps a smile of approval.

To my thinking, he held the key to my legitimacy. He was my beginning, the very stuff I was made from. My mother and grandmother had told me many times that I was conceived in love. If that was true, then meeting him, touching him, seeing him with my own eyes, would somehow enable me to know myself.

I was sure that in meeting my father, I could withdraw my illegitimate label: "The bastard shall not enter the congregation of the Lord; even to his tenth generation." All of my life, I had understood being a bastard as not belonging, not being real, not being legitimate—or, from a later biblical version of the word bastard, as being a foreigner. I recall thinking that if he would just welcome me, I would be known and therefore authenticated.

After much consideration about a course of action, I called a Catholic church near where my father lived in New York. After introducing myself to Father Joe, I explained my situation and asked him to facilitate the initial phone call that could lead to a meeting. By the grace of God—and, I suspect, Father Joe's persuasion—my father agreed to a time and place. Over the next few months, I could barely contain my eagerness. Time passed painfully slowly.

The day finally arrived. I flew from Florida to New York and met Father Joe. He jokingly told my father that he could not miss us at the restaurant since I was female, blond, and five-foot-four, and that he was six-foot-four, black, and wearing a priest's collar. I shall always be indebted to that angel of God. My anxious eyes were as large as saucers as I waited to finally set them on this man, *my father.*

Indeed, I knew at once that the man who walked through the door of the restaurant *was* my father. Much to my dismay, with eagerness strangling my initial words, I resorted to my childhood habit of stuttering. Finally, after a few pleasantries, we left Father Joe sipping a cup of coffee at the counter while we took a booth in the corner. As soon as we were seated, I instantly calmed down. About thirty minutes later, my father assured Father Joe that he could leave and that I would be escorted safely. My father and I had decided to go somewhere to have a few beers.

After sharing a large pitcher of beer, my father said as delicately as he could, "Your mother was a loose woman, and you're not my daughter, but after spending time with you tonight, I will always wish that you were." I was neither surprised, nor upset, that he had denied paternity. In my heart, I *knew* that he was my father.

As I got up to use the restroom, I looked under the table for my other shoe, and I saw that this man—this stranger who had adamantly denied paternity—was also barefoot under the table. As I lifted my head from beneath the table, I teasingly observed aloud, "Well, I see neither of us is into wearing shoes."

At that moment, our eyes met, and as God is my witness, I knew that he knew, without a doubt, that I was indeed his daughter. I also knew, in that instant, that I was free from my obsession of needing anything else from him. Our ease with one another (after some initial awkwardness), in sharing pitchers of beer, with laughter stemming from a mutual sense of humor, and coupled with his sweet tenderness, was deeply satisfying. I no longer had any doubt that I could finally let go and release this man from any further expectations I might have felt I deserved. He had given me enough.

Hours later, he drove me back to where I was staying for the night. He asked me if he could please drive me to the airport in the morning. As we sat in the driveway, I looked at him and said, "It's the alcohol talking, and you'll feel different in the morning." He insisted and I relented to his request, but in the morning I got his phone call begging forgiveness since he wouldn't be able to drive me to the airport, after all. I understood. Even knowing that I would never again see my father, I flew back to Florida feeling deeply content.

***

I would never again speak with either my grandmother or father. I don't regret any discomfort that I may have caused my father by my persistence in our meeting. He had long ago set circumstances into motion, and I was now merely playing out my part. His mother and I were the collateral damage, as it were, of his choices. Althea and I had entered into a covenant that should never have been necessary.

In my self-centered desperation, I held my grandmother emotionally hostage for some fifteen years prior to the eventual meeting with my father. I deeply regret all the distress that I caused her. She was, after all, only trying to protect her son and her grandchildren. I would have done the same. Wisdom sometimes comes only after humiliation and contrition.

Both died long ago. I can only trust that wherever my grandmother rests, she somehow understands and forgives me my trespasses.

I believe that even reluctant deeds count somewhere in time. My grandmother did a good deed every time she placed tiny nuggets, disguised as icy words, as bounty into a child's empty pan. I so want her to know that even if each phone call was nothing more than a handful of fool's gold, every minuscule amount panned from her unwilling, stiff words helped bind me to my image of my father. Someday my pan would be filled up enough so that I could separate the gold from the mud and sand of life.

***

Four years prior to meeting my father, I had a therapist who believed deeply in genetics. When I would say things like, "No, I will not give up, no matter what," he would respond, "You must get that trait from your father." Whether true or not, his opinion was relevant. I needed an idealized image of a strong parent to propel me forward through life, to affix me with a seal of authenticity. The image itself gave me hope.

After the meeting with my father, I came away feeling that he was proud of me and that if circumstances were different, he could and would be my father. That was enough confirmation to last me until I was eventually able to endorse myself.

He Calls Me High-Pockets

PERHAPS IT WAS because of the embarrassment brought on by my long-ago decayed teeth that I was obsessive about the care of my children's teeth. When the twins were two and my daughter four, I brought them for their first dental checkup. Dr. Mike was recommended by my next door neighbor, and was considered one of the best dentists in the area.

Mike was forty-three when we met, divorced once, and had a ten-year-old daughter. I was twenty-eight, and divorced twice. Several fillings later, Mike walked me to the door and said, "Would you like to go to dinner, or are you involved?" I explained that I was involved, but thanked him for his offer. He said, "You have an open invitation."

One year later, after my breakup with Bo, I called him to see if the invitation was still open. We agreed upon a time for our first date, but it was our third date that changed my life forever.

Promptly at 6:00 p.m., Mike rang the doorbell for our date. I knew by now that he would open the door of his older but sensible car for me, which I appreciated. I was not used to such gentlemanly behavior, and it really made me feel like a lady. The radio was playing soft music as we drove toward the interstate. I thought back to our second date, when we'd had a flat tire during a horrific thunderstorm. Fear knotted my stomach as I waited for the customary onslaught of anger and cursing, as was the case in all three of my past significant relationships. Instead, Mike calmly navigated the car to the side of the road, looked at me, and said, "We are so lucky to not have been on the interstate when this happened." He got out during a break in the rain and changed the tire. To my delight, his calm attitude under fire has remained consistent. He has always been easy on my mind.

I asked, "Tell me about the people who we are visiting."

"We're going to my ex-wife, Carol, and her husband Bobby's house for dinner."

As my mind ran around inside of itself looking for a familiar place to park this curious bit of information, I squeaked out something like "Oh, I see."

Mike went on, "Carol's father had a serious stroke a number of years ago. His mind is fine but he has aphasia and is unable to match the correct words to his thoughts. He's confined to the house and gets very lonely. I've played cards with Poppa once a week for years. Carol remarried about six years ago to Bobby, and he and I became good friends."

Again I mumbled something lame like, "Really, wow." As we pulled into the driveway, Mike continued with more details. "For the past three years, every other weekend, when I've picked up my daughter, Ann, for the weekend, I've taken their little daughter, Christine, as well; I have grown to love her like my own."

Forcing out my mature voice, I asked, "How old are the girls now?" "Ann is ten and Christine just turned five." Mike got out and walked around the car to open the door for me. He took my hand, and we proceeded to the front door, where we heard sounds of laughter and music.

My nervousness disappeared immediately as a beautiful woman opened the door with a hug for Mike and a most welcoming smile and an extended hand. I knew immediately that this was Carol. She was blond, slender, and abundantly gracious. Her fair skin and piercing blue eyes were stunning. As Mike headed toward the bedroom to visit with Poppa, Carol said, "Come, let me fix you a drink and introduce you to my husband, Bobby. Mike very seldom brings a friend for us to meet, so you must already be special to him."

About this time a large presence walked in with thundering laughter and some joke about Mike and me resembling the beauty and the beast. Apparently, Bobby and Mike's good-natured barbs toward one another were legendary. Bobby's success as a bartender had less to do with his good looks and everything to do with his good nature and amazing, quick wit. As Carol handed me a scotch and soda, the most delightful little blond girl bounced into the kitchen, making funny faces. I knew at once this was Christine; she appeared to be as amusing as Bobby, her father. Finally, I met a tall, slender girl with shining brown hair and a cautious stare. Ann scrutinized me with her intense brown eyes. She was the image of her father, who by now was deeply engrossed in a card game with Poppa.

Somewhere between that first handshake with Carol and her warm good-bye hug I remember thinking, *I'm really going to have to step up to the plate if I ever want to become part of this man's life*. In ways that I did not yet understand, I could see how important this family, now his family, was to him. I knew that I had to find a way to open my mind and heart to something new, something that was way outside of any traditional "norms."

Just as he cared deeply for Bobby, Poppa, and Christine, I could feel that Mike was not "in love" with Carol but that he cared for her like family. The depth of familial connection that I felt between these individuals forewarned me that if I were to be with him I had to accept them as well. As the weeks passed and I reflected on that lovely evening, I wondered about the character of a man who would volunteer to spend time without obligation with an old man who could not speak. And what kind of man would consistently take on the responsibility of an additional child for an entire weekend. A dependable man with a kind heart, I thought; perhaps the same kind of man that took responsibility for his own mistakes and who never said a bad word about his ex-wife. Shocked, I pondered this rare species of a man, which was to-tally unknown to me. On our fourth date, I marveled as he invited my mother to have dinner with us during her visit from California. I wondered with increasing interest, who *was* this incredible man?

As the holidays neared, I fretted over where to spend them. This was the first Christmas that my children had lived with their father, and I was torn between wanting to be with them and with Mike. Carol, knowing that I had no family, invited me and my children to her home for Christmas. This was the beginning of Carol's kindhearted generosity. Her goodwill would be extended to me and my children over many years to come.

Sadly, about a year after first meeting Carol, Bobby fell in love with another woman and asked Carol for a divorce. Carol was devastated and in need of some moral support and an immediate job. I was working as a life insurance agent, and my company needed a top-notch front office person. I recommended Carol, who was hired on the spot. There ensued a wonderful two-year working relationship that was frowned on by the majority, bewildered the minority, and amused us totally. We have all vacationed together, and last year Carol attended my husband's family reunion, a weeklong gathering of sixty-some people, tucked away on the shore of a huge picturesque lake in Northern Wisconsin.

Fast-forward thirty-five years, and this coming Christmas, Carol and Christine will again outdo themselves with a delicious dinner for their non-traditional family. From all directions we will spring, gathering at Christine's house. Carol's new husband will arrive with a pumpkin pie. Helping with festivities will be Christine's husband, Matt, and eight-year-old son, Matthew. Matt will serenade us with his guitar, accompanied by my husband, the "opera" star. From across the state will come Matt's mother, her husband, her ex-husband, and his new wife. Bringing good cheer will be Bobby (Christine's dad, in case you are losing track), with his usual humorous barbs for everyone, and his now-wife, Phyllis. My grandson, Zachary, will charge in with my daughter, Alex, and her husband, Andres, exhaustedly in tow. With twinkling eyes, my step-daughter, Ann, and her daughters, Cheyanne and Hanna, twenty and fifteen, will arrive. Dogs barking, eggnog flowing, aromas abounding, this family of old sorts and new sorts will greet one another with handshakes and hugs. Left unspoken are any of the tears and fears of the past; as the changing faces of "the family" transition with good cheer.

For Carol's example of magnanimity, I will forever be grateful. Some thirty-five years after she first opened her door with such grace and generosity, I am moved by her ability to forgive, include, and unite. I look forward to seeing those beautiful blue eyes every Christmas day.

Mike and I married two years after our first meeting. Our friendship blossomed into a solid and lasting connection despite our first eight years of tumultuous arguing, which was precipitated by alcohol. Mike's original open invitation remains open thirty-five years later. He tells me that he admires my grit. Growing up on a farm during the Depression years, he learned that he had to keep going no matter what the obstacle. Once, as I marched out the front door heading toward a new challenge, head down, forehead knitted into a deter-mined frown, wearing my favorite blue jeans with the big pockets, my beloved shouted, "Go get 'em, high-pockets!"

We have spent at least half of our Christmases with Mike's daughters and gracious ex-wife. I adore my husband, and I have come to deeply appreciate the complexities of blended families and our remarkable life together. This opportunity alone has stretched me into a much larger person than I could have ever imagined myself becoming. Growing up, inclusiveness was valued in my family despite its otherwise profound dysfunction. My grandmother would have been proud of me had she lived long enough to witness our family. My mother did get to witness our marriage, and was grateful that at last I was in "good hands." We combine admiration, appreciation, and respect, and nothing can be finer in a relationship. I once read a poem that expressed my heart regarding my beloved Michael:

The one I wanted came, The one I called.

Not the one who sweeps away defenseless skies, stars without homes,
moons without a country, snows.

The kind of snows that fall from a hand, a name
a dream, a face.

Not the one who tied death to his hair.
The one I wanted. Without scraping air,
Without wounding leaves or shaking windowpanes.

The one who tied silence
To his hair.

To scoop out, without hurting me,
A shoreline of sweet light inside my chest so that my soul could
sail.

The Good Angel by Rafael Alberti

After Enlightenment, Self-Responsibility

IT WAS IN August 1976 that Tom Wolfe, writing for *New York Magazine*, first used the expression "the 'me' decade" to describe the new prevailing attitude of Americans towards self-awareness and the need of fairness in the conduct of human relationships. At that time I was struggling with what I saw as a woman's dependence on men for her sense of empowerment or worth. Feelings ranging from bitter helplessness to seething anger were elicited as I became obsessed with the need to be self-supporting. Determined to never again be dependent on a man for my financial well-being became my number one goal.

Ironically, during this time, one of the most frequent commercials on television was "Mr. Coffee," featuring none other than Joe DiMaggio Sr.—my ex-father-in-law, and an all-American hero. Every time I turned on the television, I was reminded of my own self-deprecating past by the sight and sound of him, which posed a powerful challenge to my otherwise growing self-confidence. Not a rational reaction, I know, but these were my thoughts at the time.

Before I could learn to be in a healthy, interdependent relationship with a partner, I desperately needed to stop feeling subordinate to men or dependent on them for a reason to exist.

It would be some time before I felt secure enough in my own selfhood to not need the energy that anger gave me to break free of men's opinions of me. Totally absorbed in my effort to become my own person, I was ripe for any type of self-help program including the "human potential" movement. Still, it took a long time for me to understand there is a big difference between being truly independent (which always involves interdependence) and going *against* someone.

***

The year was 1977. I had recently married for the third time, but this time was the polar opposite from any relationship that I'd had before. Maybe the feminist agenda was infiltrating into my personal belief system. Whatever made the difference, this time I had married a man whose influence was positive and calming. Mike was the first man who did not make my hair stand straight up with fear every time he walked into the room.

In a bizarre twist of logic, I had deduced that Mike would never hit me, which was my one and only deal-breaker. First and foremost, I had to feel physically safe before I could proceed with "self-help/growth." The second thing that helped me relax into the relationship was a certain type of integrity (I did not have the wherewithal to name it at that point) displayed by my husband.

Driving home after a weekend holiday in the Florida Keys, I noticed

Mike was very quiet.

"What's up?" I said.

"I just feel like an idiot."

"Really? Why?"

"First, I lock my keys in the car, then I forget my shoes at the pool, and now I realize that we are just about out of gas and this is Memorial Day weekend and I am not sure that anything will be open where we can get enough gas to get home." (Thirty-five years ago, the Keys were very sparsely populated, and businesses were few and far between.)

"Wow! I think that I love you!"

"Excuse me?"

"Never mind."

I was stunned into silence as I sat beside him, thinking, *What kind of person says things like that?* I had never in my entire life heard anyone take responsibility for their mistakes. I had always been the blamed or the blamer.

Even though Mike was the single safest man I had ever known, and we had so much going for us, I was still medicating a lifetime of anxiety with alcohol two to three times a week. We had many drunken arguments. It seemed like my insides refused to stop reacting as if some untold disaster were about to happen. My need for excessive vigilance prevailed at all times. I constantly scanned the world for the next calamity.

In my previous marriages, I had internalized every negative opinion that anyone—especially my husbands—had toward me. Now I was like a heated Teflon pan, allowing nothing that sounded even slightly negative to stick to me. Unfortunately, my defensiveness was so instantaneous that I often perceived a negative motive where there were none. By the time we had been married a year, it was clear that I needed a major adjustment in my perspective on life, myself, and others.

Mike and I made the decision to sign up for a weekend seminar, or "training session," recommended to us by some friends. We signed up for something called EST. We weren't sure what it was exactly, but we were willing to learn something that might help our relationship.

In the years since the 1970s, when it was widely popular, Erhard Seminar Training (EST) has often been cited as a hallmark example of the "human potential" movement fostered by the "me" generation that inspired Tom Wolfe's article, mentioned earlier.

During a ten-year span, over one million people participated in EST training, including such celebrities as Diana Ross, Valerie Harper, and John Denver. I am aware that EST has been defined as nothing more than a self-indulgent, cult-like movement. I totally understand that perspective, because there were indeed many annoying aspects of the program: the four-day seminars (two weekends) did use a lot of extreme measures such as keeping participants in back-to-back sessions for hours without allowing the use of the bathroom. Such measures were used to break down a person's ego-defenses, though, and to open us to self examination. I know that our marriage would not have lasted had it not been for how I was affected by those weekends. My exposure to the intense self-searching eventually led to what I refer to as my first conscious moment. A defining moment, indeed!

***

"You are all assholes and don't even know that you are assholes. Your lives do not work and you don't even know that your lives are not working!" shouted the trainer standing on the stage in front of the two hundred-fifty participants the first day. The trainer's shocking method of delivery had me practically frozen to my seat in fear. I could see no reason for this woman to be what I perceived as downright mean, rude, and abusive. After just the first hour of the first day of the training, I had already sunk so low in my chair that I couldn't see over the top of the heads of those seated in front of me. Already, my only goal was simply to steel myself against the epithets she was using and *get through* the day as unnoticed as possible. Surely I could do that; after all, I was the consummate "get througher." I may be the only person who ever managed to survive a year of EST programs without ever having spoken a word.

Mike, in stark contrast to my defensiveness toward what I perceived to be an assault by the trainer, sat through the sessions unruffled and merely curious about where the training was headed. While I took every word personally, Mike did exactly the opposite. After all, the trainer wasn't saying anything Mike believed about himself. Mike didn't believe himself an asshole; not like I did, at least. While I wanted to run, Mike wanted to discern the purpose and intention of the course. Unbeknownst to either one of us at that moment, it was

Mike's quiet composure that single-handedly steadied me. He helped me sit still long enough to be awakened to how much I needed to discover and resolve in myself.

The facilitator continued to bark at us, but she also began to explain that one reason most human beings deserve to be called "assholes" is that most of us will go to any length to be *right*. In the process of being *right* you are making another person wrong, you are attacking the other person's integrity, and damaging their aliveness, and you are paradoxically doing the same to your own.

Dumbfounded, I sat there, slumped down in my seat, no longer just going along but trying to survive. All of a sudden I was hearing what was being presented. *What a humbling concept*, I thought. That way of getting through life was exactly *my* way! My entire way of interacting with Mike was exactly what the trainer had said. I always had to be right, or at least not wrong. I had to win every argument, even if it meant "out-arguing" Mike and driving him to the point of sheer exhaustion so that he would give in. Of course, this in turn gave me the false sense of satisfaction that I had won something of value. Until attending that weekend, I had never given any thought to the fact that my need to be right, no matter what the cost, was creating a growing deficit in our "communication bank account."

***

During the first three months after my participation in the EST weekends, something deep inside of me was incubating, growing—*changing*. Words and the concepts those words symbolized kept breaking through into my consciousness in moments of solitude and contemplation.

One day, as I was driving on the Florida Turnpike, I found myself reflecting on how often the EST trainer had used the terms "cause" and "effect." Cause and effect. Cause and effect. I kept saying the words over and over in my head as I drove—just as perplexed as ever at what in the world they meant—then, suddenly, *I knew*. Out of nowhere, my whole life flashed through my mind.

I saw with unmistakable clarity that I was in charge of my attitude and responses. I was in charge of how I interpreted each and every one of my life's experiences. While it was true that I had not necessarily chosen the actual circumstances I was exposed to, I was the one who held onto lifelong beliefs about every experience. They were my interpretation of the experiences. In the light of this awakening, I first saw that it was my core belief that I was hopelessly stupid which naturally ensured that I would meet and marry men who affirmed and reinforced that very self-imposed estimation of myself.

Next, my thoughts swept back through my childhood and revealed to me that while I was obviously not responsible for my abusers' words and deeds, I was responsible for the *meaning* that I had assigned to them. I was also responsible for the way I allowed my negative feelings toward men to infect my feelings toward *all* men, even Mike. The only major issue that troubled our relationship, besides alcohol, was his constant effort to correct my grammar. He thought that if he corrected me often enough, I would learn lessons obviously not picked up in school. Meanwhile, I took his correction as just one more example of what I expected from men—criticism—and assumed the worst about this part of our relationship.

As my self-protective defenses began to disintegrate, I saw I had been projecting on Mike the belief that men were untrustworthy and all but completely soulless, hardly more than a *thing* that had to be endured and managed. I saw how, from early childhood, I had internalized the belief that a man was something a woman needed for no other reason than to get by in life, like one needed currency for the exchange of goods.

Oh my God! I could hardly contain the shock that was rocking my whole paradigm of reality. I had spent my life thinking that it was the men swirling around me in the turbulence of my life that were the ones objectifying women—objectifying me! Could I have been so wrong in my beliefs? As crazy as it may sound, I was excited to see how mistaken I had been. Truly, it was one of the most thrilling moments of my life to realize that just by acknowledging and changing my beliefs I had something to say about how my life turned out. Up until that moment, I had assumed that I was like an old cork, bobbing aimlessly upon water, drifting wherever men's opinions and desires moved me.

I understood in that instant that I was not defined solely by my history or by my current circumstances. My thoughts, feelings, beliefs, and ways of relating to the world were mine and mine alone. I was absolutely free to keep, to alter, to shift, to disregard, to forget, to remember, or to forgive and let go of everything that had ever happened to me. *I was free to choose* how to define my own life story, my own reality. As my beloved grandmother would so often say, "Jesus, Mary, and Joseph!" What an exhilarating, awe-inspiring moment.

***

In 1978, Mike and I moved into a home on a little canal in Fort Lauderdale, Florida. It was there that I met Judith, the next woman to have a life-changing impact on my life. Judith lived across the street from me, and as our friendship blossomed we began to meet several mornings each week at 5:30 a.m. With coffee in hand, we drove to the beach just in time to watch the sunrise, jog, and discuss various spiritual literatures.

If it was EST that cracked opened my armor-plated heart, it was Judith's influence that replaced the confused and punitive worldview I held with one of infinite spirituality. When I learned that she was studying to be a minister, I was deeply intrigued. Spiritually, I felt like a babe just awakening and ravenously hungry.

While jogging on one of those glorious, sun-filled mornings, I was suddenly struck with a profound knowledge: that the God of my childhood understanding was *not* the God I was awakening to. That longheld image of a jealous, judgmental, controlling God who lived in a faraway sky could never again be the God of my understanding. On that hallmark morning, I came to believe that God, as Mystery, lived within each of us, inviting our participation in a direct relationship. The beauty of that moment was stunning.

Before long, Mike and I began attending classes at Judith's church, where we were introduced to "New Thought" teachings by such spiritual giants as Ralph Waldo Emerson, Thomas Troward, and Emmet Fox. Along with their writings, we studied *Varieties of Religious Experiences* by William James of Harvard University. In the midst of all of these amazing insights, I was shown the thrilling truth, once again, that I could change my very life experiences from the inside out by choosing to view the world through a different set of beliefs.

I began keeping a record of every negative thought I held about myself throughout the day, and I was shocked at how relentlessly I beat myself up over every conceivable mistake. By always expecting the worst, I attracted harmful people and thus harmful experiences to myself—or, at the very least, I diminished the potentially positive experiences I might have had. While I didn't feel I *deserved* for bad things to happen to me, I certainly had believed that if a bad thing was going to happen, it would most definitely happen to me—and all too often it did.

Within the atmosphere created by Judith and her church community, I continued to awaken to the power of my internal spiritual life. I became like a kid in a candy store. I read every metaphysical and philosophical book that I could get my hands on. As my new perspective on God and myself grew, the world began opening up in exciting ways.

Acting upon my growing sense of self-confidence and general competency, I began working as a fairly successful insurance agent. I also enrolled in night school two nights a week, working toward an associate degree in the arts. Me! I was going to college! I was emerging from a life of self-loathing and self-condemnation! Unfortunately, however, my drinking—which had served for so long as an escape—continued to haunt me, threatening to undermine my progress.

***

I did not drink every day, nor did I get drunk every time I drank. I was always surprised on those mornings that I awoke struggling to remember how I got home the night before. I would often be terrified to answer the door on those mornings, fearing that whoever I met there would somehow guess—or maybe even know—something about my shameful behavior from the night before. All this, when I had no idea if anything shameful had even happened!

During the next few years, as I finished obtaining my bachelor's degree and somehow survived four unruly teenage children, I tried hard to control my drinking. Since I did not get drunk every time I drank, I kept telling myself there was no way I was an alcoholic. Little did I realize at the time that the very fact that I was having this debate with myself was a sign that I had already slipped into the denial that is characteristic of every alcoholic. People who do not have a problem with alcohol have no reason to even enter into this kind of self-argument.

Then came the weeklong vacation that we were able to take on a friend's fifty-five-foot sailboat, anchored in the Bahamas. *Wow*, I thought. *This is going to be great. A whole week with nothing to do but putter around on the boat, relax, and drink as much as I want.* After all, what else was there to do in the lazy, sun-baked, fish-until-you-drop atmosphere onboard the boat except drink beer and Bloody Marys? Most people—at least those who thought like I did—would say, "Of course! What else! Relax, enjoy!" But, ironically, I had bought a book about alcoholism at the airport bookstore—just out of "curiosity."

So, with one beer after another in hand, I read about alcoholism over the course of that week and learned that it is a *disease*. I learned that it was not how often or how much I drank but what happened to me when I drank that made me an alcoholic. I learned that it was the way that my personality changed when I drank that mattered. I could never predict what my behavior would become after I took even just one drink. As often as not, I would become argumentative and would say and do things that were 180 degrees from what my sober self would ever say or do. Normal drinkers rarely experience those kinds of consequences when they drink alcohol.

Paradoxically, as I read, I felt two completely opposite reactions. On the one hand, I was relieved to find there was a clinical name at the root of my drinking behaviors; on the other, I was terrified. How could I ever live without being able to drink to find a few minutes of relief from my constant anxiety? I simply could not envision life without the comfort gleaned from alcohol.

I will never forget my last night of drinking. It happened on that sailboat, on a gorgeous evening in which we had invited the people on the boat next to ours to join us for dinner. I guess it's kind of funny for me to say I will never forget that night, because the truth is, I only remember our guests coming aboard and then leaving. I remember absolutely nothing in between. When I awoke the next morning I had to wait for my husband to awaken so that I could try and read his face. Had I embarrassed him? Had I done anything outrageous? Was he mad at me?

When he finally awoke, he appeared fine, his usual, happy-go-lucky self. I was too ashamed to tell him that I couldn't remember anything. I tried to discreetly ask him about the evening. He said that we all had a good time and that I was funny and engaging. Funny? Engaging? Thank God! And I couldn't remember a moment of it. I was utterly confused, mainly because I had yet to learn that when an alcoholic has a blackout they can appear to be totally conscious to others. Years ago there were stories of pilots flying planes in a blackout. I had always thought blackout meant the person passed out. I knew then that I was done with drinking, but I could not imagine how I would accomplish quitting.

Oh, the ironies of life. In two weeks, I was to start my internship at a Woman's Alcohol Recovery Center. Working toward my master's degree in social work, I had been given the choice between an internship working with battered women or alcoholic women. I had chosen what I thought to be the lesser of two painful situations. Afraid of losing this much sought after internship, I was determined to never reveal my own drinking problem.

I was so moved by the honesty of the women at this agency that I walked into my supervisor's office the very first afternoon, my chin quivering with fright, a little drool sliding down my chin, and said, "I have a problem with alcohol." My supervisor, Karen, started laughing. She looked at me with more compassion that I had ever seen in my life and said, "God sure has brought you to the right place; I believe there are no accidents." Tears streamed down my face as I thanked her. Then she sent me into the group room to lead groups, since I had formal training in group dynamics. I showed movies on alcoholism as a family disease. Trying to hide my tears during these movies was a challenge that I did not always meet. It was quite a humbling experience when my clients suggested that I attend some meetings for myself.

Shortly thereafter, I became a member of a fellowship that helped people with alcohol problems. Mike chose to give up drinking about a week later. In the fellowship of my newfound friends, I found support in putting into action all of the amazing spiritual truths I had been learning over the past seven years. It was here that I learned to extend to others the forgiveness and love I felt from the God I had recently come to understand. After all the years I heard my grandmother recite "Our Father," I learned what it actually meant to forgive my trespassers and to feel forgiven for my own trespasses. I began to see that all of us, without exception, have both received hurt *from* and inflicted hurt *on* another.

But First the Amends

"I dreamed I had a child, and even in the dream I saw it
was my life, and it was an idiot, and I ran away. But it
always crept on to my lap again, clutched at my clothes.
Until I thought, if I could kiss it, whatever in it was my
own, perhaps I could sleep. And I bent to its broken
face, and it was horrible…but I kissed it. I think one
must finally take one's life in one's arms, Quentin."

—Arthur Miller

WHEN I FIRST heard people talk about amends to those we had
harmed, especially our ex-spouses, I thought they must be crazy. Erro-
neously, I believed that if my tormentors' transgressions outweighed
mine, my "sin" was somehow diminished, even canceled. For example,
I thought if people knew how cruel my ex-husband had been toward me
and our children, they would see how righteous I had been. That
should exempt me from making amends to him, right? But—au contraire—I had to take responsibility for my own sins of omission and
commission without defenses or excuses. Grudgingly at first, I began to
think about who I was and what I was like when Bill and I married.
What exactly did I—a frightened, needy, nearly delirious young girl—
bring to the marriage? The answer was nothing. Absolutely nothing! I
realized that while he was marrying me for his own reasons, I had married him to escape my love for and rage at Joey. I used what many would
consider a sacred act—the sacrament of marriage—to arrest my descent
into booze and promiscuity.

Driven by self-destructive beliefs, alcohol was my comfort, my only
defense—my fortress against the ghosts and monsters of my "sins." But
my liquid comfort would eventually turn on me, causing me to lose my
dream job as a stewardess, much the way drugs and alcohol played a
major role in the demise of Marilyn. Under its influence I could forget
that I was not supposed to want too much out of life or expect too little. But in its clutches of insanity, I wanted everything and nothing all
at once. I had married Bill and brought my nineteen-year-old self—an
empty satchel stuffed with pain—to my second marriage. I appropri-
ated him to escape my internal barbarians and shameful acting-out
behaviors.

So I wrote Bill a letter of apology. In the letter I revealed my
shameful secrets to him. I told him how my choices culminated in the
brutal rape and suicide attempt just months prior to our marriage. I

apologized for having nothing to contribute to our years together except fear and emptiness. I asked his forgiveness. I had to let go of any concern about how he would respond. The release that came to me after mailing that letter was like a huge stone melting away.

When Bill died four years ago, I was able to facilitate my children's grief and farewells. By their own choice they had not spoken with him in several years, but I felt that grieving his passing was paramount to their healing journey. We lit candles and wished him well on his crossing. They whispered their regrets. I felt blessed to have been given such softness in my heart toward him.

My children no longer had to carry the heavy stone of family wounds heaped upon them by their parents.

Unhealed wounds have a way of becoming like family legacies; burdens that keep on giving down through the generations. Esteemed Pulitzer Prize recipient Ernest Becker notes that the young child automatically and unthinkingly absorbs parts of her primary caretakers' world views, that "each of us in some way is a grotesque collage, a composite of injected and ejected parts over which we have no honest control." Psychologists refer to these parts by many names: ego states, sub-selves, shadow parts, the child within, etc.

Watching my children tend to their "father wounds" reminded me of a similar process with my father.

Howard died alone in the dilapidated trailer shortly after his wife, Vi, died from alcoholism. When they found him beneath the sagging tin roof, which was draped with a filthy black tarp to keep out the rain, dozens of empty booze bottles lay scattered at his feet.

Howard and my mom had been divorced for many years at the time of his death, but she saw to it that he had a military burial. I remain in awe of the generosity of spirit that she alone extended to Howard by arranging his funeral.

Grandma Kelley, my adoptive father's mother, had been dismayed at the change in her son's behavior when he returned from overseas. She said that the war had changed him beyond recognition. She told me that he had witnessed the deaths of his entire platoon, which was blown up before his eyes. He was their sergeant and the only survivor. He was awarded medals for acts of bravery and valor—a secret that he took to his grave, never even discussing it with his family. His medals, discovered by my mother, were among his few belongings. One can only imagine his lingering inner turmoil.

Post-traumatic stress disorder was not a commonly acknowledged symptom of war in the mid-1940s. Who but those who have shared a similar experience could possibly imagine the demons that dwell in a human heart and mind after witnessing, perhaps even participating, in such horror?

I am sorry now that Howard lived and died alone. I am even sorrier that he suffered his internal torments alone; hiding the medals of honor and bravery that were awarded for acts that engendered his nightmares and perhaps precipitated his subsequent abusive behaviors.

Dear Howard,

The time came when I needed to ask God to forgive the unforgivable within me. Perhaps it was then that I learned to forgive you. Or maybe some of the forgiveness I feel now came when I participated in a therapy session in which I enacted a scene between you and me. It was the time that you tethered me to the floor in the bedroom with orange and blue linoleum tiles. Remembering it and reliving it through the power of psychodrama, I was able to reclaim the child part of myself that was metaphorically nailed to the floor. I was also able to tenderly place you into the arms of an angel for safekeeping.

I don't know if you are in a place like that now—safe, where angels abound. I hope so. Wherever your spirit may be, I want you to know that your life was not lived in vain. While there were times like the scene in the bedroom, there were also the contributions you made to my life. You took on a family of four when you were but a young man of twenty-four. You gave me your name and relieved me of some of the shame of my birth. You taught me to see the subtleties of love given in small moments, like when I watched your eyes reflected in the prism of the countless milk bottles you hauled in and stacked so carefully in that old fridge. It is true that you eventually chose a different kind of bottle to calm your internal minefields; but how could I ever blame you? The same bottles eventually became my harshest teacher as well.

The medals found at your death spoke much of the legacy that you bequeathed. You aided in the freedom that millions derive and benefit from in the world today. Thanks, Dad, for giving all that you gave. All that no one thought to remember. Dad. I feel blessed to call you that— Dad. May you now rest in peace.

Your daughter, Dawn

***

And, finally, there is my mother. Looking at the wake of destruction that I've created in my own life, how have I dared to critique her so harshly? I am ashamed of my judgments and condemnations. She lived beneath the shadow of a saint, my grandmother, who kept her head in the mystical clouds while my mother kept hers mired in the demanding drudgeries of daily life. My mother is an unsung hero. She supplied the safety net that supported our tattered lives.

Envelopes

I HAD NOT seen my mother in five years. Her visit was going well; then, out of the blue, without asking me how I might feel about it, she proclaimed, "Dawn, when I get back to San Diego I'm going to pack up everything and move here. I would love to live in this town."

Alarm bells screaming in my ears, I said, "Oh, Mom! I don't think that is a good idea—after living in San Diego all of these years, you will miss the sun and the warmth. It gets really cold here, Mom. The Pacific Northwest is known worldwide for its long, rainy days."

"I'll be fine, Honey."

"Mom! Mom, you just don't understand. From fall through winter it often gets dark as early as 3:30 in the afternoon. You would hate it."

"I won't care one bit; besides, I will have you!"

Panic threatened to overwhelm me. Slowly shriveling inside, I continued trying to dissuade her from her flippant wish to slither into my safe haven.

"You won't have me, Mom, I am very busy with work, trainings, meetings, and traveling. I will not be able to be there for you. Mom, this is not a good idea." With that faraway look she got when she had gone to a place that I couldn't reach, she simply said, "It will take me a week."

After crying most of the next week in utter despair, I found myself driving a U-Haul from San Diego to my home and helping my mother move into her new low-income housing apartment.

***

My mother and I had ten years together. I was glad to have been able to give her everything but my heart. She slid into my life, but not into my pocket, as she would have preferred. After living nearby for three months and expecting me to cater to her every need, we had one of those "come to Jesus" conversations.

I said, "Mom, it looks to me like you want to die!" "What is that supposed to mean?" she asked.

"Well, you are unwilling to follow any of the doctor's recommendations; you will not take care of your diabetes or exercise or make friends or even leave your apartment, for that matter."

With dripping sarcasm, she said, "What are you, my daughter the therapist?"

Letting that remark slide, I said, "I'm just saying, if you are simply waiting to die, I will help you get your things in order—but after that, I am absolutely not willing to make you my life project."

My mother slammed into the bathroom, and I left her apartment. Two days later, she began getting herself a life. She found the little bus that stopped at her building complex. Three times a week she went swimming at our local, Olympic-size pool. She began walking. I helped her find a doctor, bought her some beautiful velvet jogging suits, and taught her how to brush her hair straight back into a ponytail, holding it in place with the beautiful bows that I had made for her. She looked elegant. My lady friends graciously included her in all of our lunches, and she actually began working at a twelve-step program.

Ten years later, my mother died softly in my arms. My dear friend Marjorie and I prayed as many Catholic prayers as we remembered to comfort her onward into the light. It was beautiful. I keep my mother's picture on my prayer table, just under my grandmother's Mary, Mother of God statue. One day while in prayer and meditation, I recalled that long ago day when my mother purchased the statue.

The year was 1952; I was seven years old. I could feel my mother tingling with excitement as we entered the five-and-ten-cent department store. My mother had painstakingly put aside scarce household change in anticipation of this day. She was buying a Mother of God statue for her spiritually devout mother.

My grandmother wept with joy at the sight of her beloved Mary statue. It was a rare day of celebration, with each of us allotted an extra bowl of potato soup and a glass of powdered milk.

My mind snapped back to the present. Mysteriously, in one blessed moment, I was able to finally give my heart to my mother—the one thing she had most wanted.

> My mother, my mother, how sorry my heart for judging you, misconstruing you, condemning you.
>
> My heart tethered to your mother, my grandmother, she the quintessential saint, you the offender. She proclaimed absolute trust in divinity while you begged for understanding the tangible, bent over small, empty envelopes, agonizing how to fill each with the debtors share.
>
> Now and then a wayward husband or two passing through, but accountability no choice for you, three children and a dependent mother to endure caused bent shoulders, shuffling envelopes with their due.

After you passed, meticulous ledger books thinned with frayed pages revealed; two dollars toward food, five dollars for rent, one dollar toward Sears and Roebucks, small change for stamps and the church collection plates. Oh how I finally saw you!

My mother, my mother, how sorry my heart for judging you, accusing you, rejecting you.

In exchange for morsels of food you withheld, buying grandmother's cigarettes. Oh how evil of you, we children angrily spewed. Evidence of your meanness, didn't you see. Bitter, you sent us to bed without our only sustenance of day-old bread.

Your tired eyes and weary shoulders scraped and saved leftover change to buy Grandmother her coveted Mary, Mother of God statue. Oh how long and at what sacrifice did you endure for the pennies you selflessly shored? Arraigned with little faith, you doggedly accepted her blind devotion while you staggered sleepless nights, seeking solutions to our tangible hunger.

Was there ever time for healing your burdens Mother, Oh Mother, the ones that made your shoulders stoop? Your father died when you were but a child. You shouldered your orphaned, agoraphobic mother until the day that she expired. Your unrequited love left you impregnated with his bastard child and your mortal sin. Your Church rebuked you. First husband claimed by war, second husband by madness from the war, alcohol and an affair. Third husband bore the war, rendered childlike, conspired with trusted friend to embezzle your business. Debtors claimed your small treasures. Welfare system trampled you and Valium engulfed you. Your children forsook you, cancer buried you.

My Mother, my mother, how sorry my heart for judging you, accusing you, rejecting you, for it was a lifetime of haunting envelopes that frayed, stooped, and engulfed you. Rest now, Mother, as God's grace envelopes you.

Ragdoll Redeemed

BRAZILIAN CHERRY HARDWOOD floors are known for their hardness and durability. Not a day passes without a sigh of joy as my bare feet touch my beautiful hardwood floors. Independent of the temperature or seasons, the floor remains inviting beneath my feet. The richness of color offers both the elegance of time-honored solidness and the down-to-earth casualness in which I am the most comfortable.

In my wildest dreams I could not have imagined that a floor would give me such endless pleasure, since I am a person who doesn't normally attach to houses, furniture, or cars. When one steps into the living room of my Pacific Northwest home, their eyes will eventually gravitate to the view directly beyond the front door. One will notice the beautiful Strait of San Juan de Fuca bringing the Pacific Ocean to Puget Sound. And on a clear day, one will also see the San Juan Islands in the distance, and perhaps a freighter or two heading out to the East from Seattle. A spectacular view indeed, yet it is the beauty of the Brazilian cherry floors that seems to command the first attention of visitors.

Actually, I love everything about the area where I live. Pilots sometimes refer to this region as the "Blue Hole" or the "Banana Belt" of the Pacific Northwest because we only get about seventeen inches of rain per year. The glorious Olympic Mountains are to my south, usually snow-capped, providing endless enjoyment as I drive into town. To the north, just beyond the Straits (a short ferry ride away), is Victoria, Canada. On a clear day I can see—with breathtaking awe—spectacular Mount Baker, which is part of the Cascade Mountain range, to the east. Deer, hawks, eagles, and our very own herd of elk grace our community.

If all of this splendor were not enough to spread joy to my heart, then imagine the smell of fresh-cut alfalfa, clover, and timothy. Twice a year, the farmers bale hay. The huge bales lie in the fields, touching upon the perennial ritual of timelessness, with the vast view of the mountains in the background. Absorbing all of this beauty, I often feel as if my heart will burst with gratitude.

Knowing from whence I came, I have a friend that often remarks incredulously, "Dawn, you just can't get here from there." But I did! I have arrived in the winter of my life far exceeding any expectations that I might have imagined. In particular, when my friend refers to *there*, he is referring to being in a place of profound ignorance, devoid of normal maturation processes, and replete with multiple abuses. Paradoxically, these experiences were the impetus for all that I am today.

Shortly after hearing of Joey's death in 1999, during a psychodrama training class, I asked someone to role-play Joey. I wanted to give shape and form to the haunting feelings still lingering in my heart.

I gently sat the person I had chosen to portray Joey in a chair and wrapped a beautiful Native American blanket around his shoulders. Then I placed a large, red, round object in his hands to represent my heart. Sobbing, I knelt before him and thanked him for the contribution he made to my life and my spiritual growth. My unrequited love for him kept my feet firmly on a path of healing. I realized then that it was not he who stole my heart. No, it was I who had velcroed my heart to him. After some time in silence, similar to a soul retrieval, I gently took the part that represented my heart from his hands and held it to my chest, breathing in its strength as I welcomed that part of myself home.

In a beautiful ritual, my colleagues cleansed us with the ancient ritual of healing smoke from sweet grass as someone softly drummed in the background. Time and space were suspended within that sacred moment. I swear, I felt Joey's love and forgiveness embrace me as well.

I have returned full circle to that seven-year-old, tattered child who hid in the comforting arms of a eucalyptus tree. I no longer have sap on my feet or lice in my hair but every day I long for my bare feet, old, comfortable clothing—yes, some are even tattered—and the solitude of my own floors. At age sixty-six, I feel very much like the little "ragamuffin" child my grandmother used to call me.

I have to smile when I think that, six decades later, that word still grounds me in the humble, unpretentious faith in life that she modeled for me. With no effort at all, I can close my eyes and return to those childhood years when I would sit with my grandmother as she patiently sewed and patched my dumpster dolls together with her gnarled hands, using pieces of old, stained sheets. And always looking down on us from her altar were the statues of Jesus, Mary, and Joseph. And every night, there was my grandmother, standing, arms outstretched, before her beloved Mary, Mother of God statue in particular, with her rosary beads spilling from the five-pocket apron that she wore like a nun's habit. And there was the seemingly endless supply of holy water that she sprinkled nightly upon my forehead, as well as upon any of the salvaged dolls I cherished—even as Grandma cherished me. Joining each other in peals of girlish laughter as we sat on our twin beds, knees touching, smoking Kool cigarettes and trying to outdo each other at blowing the perfect smoke ring. These are the memories that remain alive deep in my heart. These were sacred moments. Moments filled with a sense of a God most high—high enough and big enough to take all the parts of life and make a whole. Those were the things that wove me whole; they were my daily morsels of bread, and I was indeed sustained.

Many years have passed since Grandmother left us. I now have my own prayer table. The Mary statue graces the center of my own "altar." Her original, beautiful colors have faded, and she has been broken and reglued more times than I can count. She is discolored, disfigured, and just plain old. But she has not lost any of the power my grandmother's nightly prayers instilled in her to perform miracles, hear prayers, and empower a believer with holy energy. Every time I look at her I feel the bountiful endowment of God's grace, the myriad of unending prayers. Some of sorrow and others of comfort, peace and gratitude, poured out before her presence by my grandmother. One day, when I pass on, perhaps this humble and rather pitiful-appearing treasure will end up in a heap in some obscure place, but the comfort that her presence has bestowed on the young and old can never be diminished.

No matter how many faces life has sewn upon the ragamuffin I am, they are all still only aspects of the *self* that I have become. Just as I used to assign personas and roles to rag dolls in the hours of make-believe, so life has assigned me many roles: bastard child, daughter, granddaughter, halfsister, white trash, ward of the state, foster child, retard, good girl/bad girl, whore, wife, ex-wife, stewardess, mother, stepmother, grandmother, student, graduate, citizen, alcoholic, victim, perpetrator, professional woman, psychotherapist, adjunct professor, friend, colleague, cancer survivor, cancer-thriver, wise woman, and crone. Even so, even now, when I have moments that *I* feel gnarled and broken, unraveled and undone, I can still sit before my own prayer table and imagine the soothing touch of my grandmother's hands sewing me back together again.

Now that I am old like the Mary statue, my essential self far exceeds the masks that I have worn.

How sad I feel when I read quotes by Marilyn (or should I call her Norma Jeane?). Her words indicate that she never got to experience her own deep longing for redemption. Instead, she was left with only her masks and the roles she felt required to fill.

> "I kept driving past the theatre with my name on the marquee. Was I excited. I wished they were using 'Norma Jeane so that all the kids at the home and schools who never noticed me could see it."
>
> — Marilyn

She was a famous movie star, yet she craved a sort of redemption, longing for recognition and admiration from those who had ignored her in her childhood. I hope that wherever Marilyn now rests, she knows that her redemption lives on in the adulation of millions who are still mesmerized by her brief life in this world. Shimmering like a candle in the wind; a candle that made life shine brighter for so many. I believe that the fundamental essence of Marilyn, of all of us, is neither created nor destroyed, but exists in timelessness, forever tethered to the mystery of God. I believe that the essence of the many *selves* that Marilyn, Joey, and I lived remains woven together like a tapestry. Despite Marilyn's demons, her contribution to the tapestry of life is legendary. Joey, at fifty-seven, also surrendered to an isolated life and premature death, facilitated by booze and pills. Yet his legacy lives on in the daughters that he adopted and who became such a source of joy to Joey's father, Joe Sr.

Joey exposed me to a whole new world of possibilities, for which I will be forever grateful. I can only hope that the threads of my life will extend far and wide and add to the beauty of this unfolding tapestry. We cannot help but leave indelible footprints on the hearts of those who have loved us. I pray that my own lingering footprints will rest lightly.

My longed-for redemption never came in any of the ways that I had imagined it would. Not one of those relationships with others that I thought might redeem me ever fulfilled that craving in the depth of my soul. Yet, somehow—through the patching and weaving together of all these lives—it has been done. I look into a mirror, into my own eyes, and see that redemption has come. I live and thrive encircled in the certainty that I am completely and unconditionally redeemed. Curiously, this redeemed state of soul has not erased all my frailties and weaknesses. I am still as imperfect a human being as it is possible to be, but with one extraordinary change: I now see, that after all my desperate pursuits of a "pardon" from life, it has been in coming home to myself and rejoicing in the diversity of me that I am redeemed. Finally, I know that the many-sided prism that I have come to recognize in myself is the totality of the me I was intended to be.

Today, I see that through all the years and all the relationships and all the parts I've played and roles I've filled, I am still the "ragamuffin" who loves simple, filling, cheap foods like mashed potatoes with mounds of butter and a glass of cold milk. But I am a rich ragamuffin—rich in the horrors and the blessings that have been the mold from which I have been formed.

Even now, as I finish this story of my quest for acceptance and redemption, Mary sits just a few feet away, holding out her arms in a gesture that invites me to surrender myself into her love, just as Grandma used to do during her nightly prayer ritual. The light is caught in the prisms of the glass beads of my grandma's rosary where it hangs, draped around Mary's neck. I love them—the rosary, the statue, and Grandmother's memory. And I love red lipstick and cleavage, even though cancer left me with only one breast to push up and show off. Broken rag doll, patched and finally loved by *me*, I am—*Jesus, Mary, and Joseph!*—truly redeemed at last.

About the Author

DAWN DELISA NOVOTNY, MSW, LCSW, MTS, CDP, CP, is a clinician, teacher, author, spiritual director, and national workshop leader with a private practice in Sequim, Washington. Novotny holds a master's degree in clinical social work. She completed a post-graduate program in Spiritual Direction sponsored by the Jubilee Community for Justice and Peace and the Vancouver School of Theology. She was an adjunct professor at Seattle University and past instructor at Peninsula Community College. She is a nationally certified psycho-dramatist and completed the advanced Internal Family Systems training in 2004.

Acknowledgements

THIS BOOK WOULD not have been possible without the loving support, guidance, and encouragement of Linda Joy Myers, Ph.D., MFT, President and Founder of the National Association of Memoir Writers and author of seven books, including *The Power of Memoir* and *Becoming Whole: Writing Your Healing Story*.

I am deeply grateful to Colleen Harrison, author of *He Did Deliver Me from Bondage: Using the Book of Mormon and the Principles of the Gospel of Jesus Christ as they correlate with the Twelve-Step Program to Overcome Compulsive/Addictive Behavior*. Her organizing, editing, and encouragement were contagious.

For the graciousness extended by Gloria Steinem's office for permission to use excerpts from her book *Marilyn*, many thanks.

Thank you to Cynthia for the cover design.

My heart is full of tender words rendered by my brother, Ron Kelley, who helped with much of the editing even as he wept through parts of our childhood memories.

A special thanks to my longtime friends, Margery Lamoroux and Nancy Nave, for their support, love, and early contributions to my writings.

Thanks also to Susan Eiland for her enthusiasm, sustained support, and belief in me.

For her sharp eye in editing and suggested chapter arrangement, many thanks to Lucy Bodilly.

I deeply appreciate the members of my writing group, Rev. Judith Churchman and Helen Lowery. First and foremost for our enduring friendship, then for their never-ending encouragement as I shared some of the most painful and embarrassing experiences of my life. I extend gratitude for repeatedly reading, commenting, and supporting my writing efforts, especially in the beginning.

To my friend and colleague, Jeanette Rodriguez, Ph.D., who is a professor in the Department of Theology and Religious Studies at Seattle University and the author of *Cultural Memory: Resistance, Faith, and Identity. Stories We Live/Cuentos Que Vivimos*, and *Our Lady of Guadalupe: Faith and Empowerment among Mexican-American Women*— our earlier writings for *The Story Teller Within: Fast Feet and Little Fingers* were, in part, the impetus for this book.

Thank you Richard Ben Cramer, author of *Joe DiMaggio, The Hero's Life*, for our lengthy phone conversation some years ago. Finally, my memories were validated.

With deep appreciation to Sue, Joey's second wife, for the generosity that you extended so long ago in that one brief phone conversation; it soothed my grieving heart. May God bless you.

Huge thanks to Robin Sim for her support, critical eye, and last-minute edits.

Boundless appreciation to my beloved husband, Dr. Milo Novotny, D.D.S., for his unending love and support, without which my stability of mind and heart might never have been possible. Thank you for being my best life choice.

Notes and Sources

STORIES PASSED DOWN by family members, memories of emotional experiences, and various conversations have been reproduced to the closest recollection of the author's ability. Some names have been changed to protect the privacy and/or anonymity of the people involved.

For quotes by Marilyn throughout this book, see:

Steinem, Gloria and George Barris. *Marilyn*. New York: East Toledo Productions, 1986).

Rosten, Norman. *Marilyn: An Untold Story*. New York: The New American Library, 1967, 1972, 1973.

All Biblical references: *The King James Bible* (old and new versions).

Chapter 1

Celani, David. *The Illusion of Love*. New York: Columbia University Press, 1994.

Chapter 2

Longfellow, Henry Wadsworth. "Table-Talk." First published in the Blue and Gold edition of *Drift-Wood*, 1857.

Chapter 16

Baseball Almanac. 11400 SW 40 Terrace, Miami, FL. 333165-4605 (Permission granted)

Chapter 24

Cramer, Ben Richard. *Joe DiMaggio, The Hero's Life*. New York: Simon & Schuster, 2000.
[quoted from *My Remarkable Journey*, by Larry King] Permission requested from Larry King.

Chapter 25

Bly, Robert. "The Long Bag We Drag Behind Us." In *A Little Book on the Human Shadow*. New York: HarperCollins Publishing, 1988.

Chapter 28

Alberti, Rafael. "The Good Angel." Fundacion@rafaelalbert.es/eng

Chapter 30

Becker, Ernest. *The Birth and Death of Meaning*. New York: The Free Press, 1971.
Miller, Arthur. *After the Fall*. New York: Bantam Books, 1965.

Photo Credits

Cover

Picture of Marilyn Monroe: Self-made screen capture from a public domain film trailer for *The Misfits* (1961). Licensing information, Creativeclearance.com.

"Picture of Joe DiMaggio and Son at Marilyn Monroe's Funeral."
© Keystone-France/Getty Images.

All other photos are the personal property of Dawn D. Novotny.

CPSIA information can be obtained at www.ICGtesting.com
Printed in the USA
BVOW070252130412

287604BV00001B/5/P